Praise for *The Front-Line Leader*

"*The Front-Line Leader* by Chris Van Gorder is a profoundly straightforward and commonsense approach to effective leadership. Chris is a leader who exemplifies the content of this book. The chapters exude wisdom that can be utilized by any discipline or profession. I saw his leadership ability first hand when during Katrina our nation needed additional resources to manage this unprecedented catastrophe. It was Chris who stepped up and successfully led a very large Scripps team to oversee the care and evacuation of thousands of victims of the Katrina disaster. I would strongly recommend this book to both seasoned and aspiring leaders, for it will challenge you to take your leadership to the next level."

—**Richard Carmona**, RN, MD, MPH, FACS,
17th Surgeon General of the United States

"As a leader, developing an employee-focused work culture is a challenge that requires daily attention and effort. In *The Front-Line Leader*, Chris Van Gorder outlines a set of practical, easily implemented strategies for leaders at every level to stay connected to their workforce. Having worked with Chris directly in his role at Scripps, and having been a patient at Scripps, I have seen first hand how this approach works. Success, whether in baseball or in business, requires a team mentality, shared commitment to a common goal, and the daily practice of winning strategies."

—**Mike Dee**, CEO, San Diego Padres

"For the past eight years, I have had the extraordinary privilege of working for Chris Van Gorder, who is not just an exemplary leader in American health care but responsible for the dramatic turnaround of Scripps Health to make it one of the best health systems in the world. In *The Front-Line Leader*, Chris shares his successful philosophy for transforming an organization from the ground up."

—**Eric Topol**, MD, chief academic officer, Scripps Health; author,
The Creative Destruction of Medicine

"Chris Van Gorder is a man of service and purpose. When disaster strikes, Chris refuses to collaborate with hopelessness but rather confronts affliction with action. Like so many great leaders, Chris has built sustainable infrastructure one front-line leader at a time, sending messages to the future that reflect his values and health care's endowed promise of a better life for all."

—**John Bardis**, president and CEO, MedAssets

"The title of *The Front-Line Leader* says it all. Chris Van Gorder's message may seem simple, but that's just the point. In this rapidly evolving tech world, it's easy to forget the basics. It doesn't matter what business you're in; Van Gorder's genuine life and business experiences will lead you to the front."

—**T. Denny Sanford**, philanthropist and chairman,
United National Corporation

"At the San Diego Sheriff's Department, we know first hand the effectiveness of Chris's front-line leadership model. He leads our Reserve Deputy Sheriff program and our volunteer Search and Rescue team, an effort that takes him into the mountains, canyons, and desert to look for folks who have lost their way. Success or failure can mean life or death. Chris Van Gorder's leadership is direct and straightforward, and so is *The Front-Line Leader*. He shows the way to become a leader who has real impact on your organization and in the lives of those around you."

—**Bill Gore**, sheriff, San Diego County

THE FRONT-LINE LEADER

BUILDING A HIGH-PERFORMANCE ORGANIZATION FROM THE GROUND UP

Chris Van Gorder

JB JOSSEY-BASS™

A Wiley Brand

Cover Design: Wiley
Cover Image : © iStock.com/francisblack

Published by Jossey-Bass
A Wiley Brand
One Montgomery Street, Suite 1200, San Francisco, CA 94104-4594
www.josseybass.com

Jossey-Bass books and products are available through most bookstores. To contact Jossey-Bass directly call our Customer Care Department within the U.S. at 800-956-7739, outside the U.S. at 317-572-3986, or fax 317-572-4002.

Wiley publishes in a variety of print and electronic formats and by print-on-demand. Some material included with standard print versions of this book may not be included in e-books or in print-on-demand. If this book refers to media such as a CD or DVD that is not included in the version you purchased, you may download this material at http://booksupport.wiley.com. For more information about Wiley products, visit www.wiley.com.

Library of Congress Cataloging-in-Publication Data
Van Gorder, Chris.
  The front-line leader : building a high-performance organization from the ground up / Chris Van Gorder.
     pages cm
  Includes index.
   ISBN 978-1-118-93334-3 (hardback); ISBN 978-1-118-93335-0 (pdf); ISBN 978-1-118-93336-7 (epub)
  1. Leadership. 2. Corporate culture. 3. Communication in organizations. I. Title.
  HD57.7.V3597 2014
  658.4'092–dc23

                                                                          2014025446

Printed in the United States of America

FIRST EDITION

HB Printing 10 9 8 7 6 5 4 3 2 1

To Rosemary, David, and Michael

Contents

Acknowledgments

I've often said that I have had the fortune and blessing of "falling up." The truth is, nobody falls up by him- or herself.

Lorin Rees of Boston's Rees Literary Agency contacted me and encouraged me to write a proposal for this book. He put me in touch with a professional writer, Seth Schulman of the Providence Word and Thought Company. With Seth's guidance, support, and writing skills, I was able to get my ideas and stories down on paper. We secured the participation of a top publisher, Jossey-Bass, and its senior editor for business, leadership, and management, Karen Murphy. I wish to express my sincere gratitude to this core team for their help and encouragement.

I am deeply grateful to many other people who also supported the writing of this book, including my immediate family—Rosemary, David, and Michael—and my extended family, the employees and physicians of Scripps Health, and my teammates in the San Diego County Sheriff's Department. I owe a debt of gratitude as well to my colleagues, friends, and editing team at Scripps Health, June Komar, Elliot Kushell, Ph.D., and Don Stanziano; our organization's senior team, Richard Rothberger, Vic Buzachero, June Komar, John Engle, Richard Sheridan, Jim LaBelle, M.D., Tom Gammiere, Gary Fybel, Robin Brown, Carl Etter, Rick Neale, Shiraz Fagan, Barbara Price, Glen Mueller, and Marc Reynolds; Scripps Chief Medical Officer Emeritus Brent Eastman, M.D.; the many members and alumni of the Scripps

Leadership Academy and Scripps Employee 100; and physician leaders at Scripps.

I'd especially like to thank the Scripps Health Board of Trustees, for whom I've had the honor of working these past fifteen years. Their leadership, guidance, encouragement, and constructive feedback are unmatched anywhere in health care. Thank you as well to the other organizations and individuals who have also contributed to the experiences described in this book: the Monterey Park Police Department, the San Diego County Sheriff's Department, the Price School of Public Policy at the University of Southern California, the California Emergency Medical Services Authority, the United States Public Health Services, Surgeon General Richard Carmona, M.D., and the American College of Healthcare Executives.

Finally, I seek to honor my deceased parents, Harold and Mary, for their love and support and for instilling the ethics and principles on which this book is based.

Introduction

In 1973, I was a hospital security officer working the graveyard shift in the basement. One night when I was the only one on duty, it was lonely and dead quiet, until I heard the sound of approaching footsteps. I looked up to see a man walking toward me. It was the CEO of my hospital. I had never met him before, but I had seen his picture; as a security officer, I was expected to know the administrators by sight.

Who knew what the CEO was doing walking around in the basement at that ungodly hour, but it didn't matter: This was my chance to meet the big boss. I thought how cool it would be to chat a little bit, make a connection. I grew up under modest circumstances in nearby Alhambra, and I knew this CEO lived in San Marino. As a teenager I had delivered newspapers in the same plush, upscale neighborhood where the CEO now lived.

Checking first to make sure my uniform was crisp, I straightened my posture and cleared my throat, readying to say hello and shake the man's hand. Instead, the CEO walked right by me, like I didn't even exist. Without making eye contact or even acknowledging my presence in that empty hallway, he turned the corner and was gone.

It was a demoralizing moment, one that clearly I have never forgotten, but it helped shape me and my views on being both an employee and a leader. That CEO saw me as "only" a security guard, but if a crime were being committed, who would have intervened? I would have, which would have made me, at that particular moment, among the hospital's most important employees. An organization's first priority, I reasoned, was to take care of its customers, and front-line staff were the ones doing that work. I resolved that if I ever took on a leadership role, I would remember this and treat employees accordingly.

I've since had that chance. After college, I went into law enforcement and spent several exciting years on the front lines as a police officer. When a devastating on-the-job injury ended my police career prematurely, I had to find a new path, so I went back to school to get a graduate degree in health care management. Over four decades I have served as a clerk in an emergency room, a manager of a hospital lab, and in higher-level management and leadership roles at several California hospitals.

In 2000 I became president and CEO at Scripps Health, one of America's most prestigious health systems. Since then my team has presided over the most dramatic turnaround in the organization's history, catapulting Scripps from near-bankruptcy to a dominant market position. While hospitals and health systems nationwide have laid people off or closed their doors, we've become financially healthy and added almost five thousand employees. Facilities in our system routinely appear in the *U.S. News & World Report* ranking of America's best hospitals. In 2014, we opened a $220 million proton therapy center, one of only a few cancer treatment centers of its kind in the United States. We also continued building a $450 million cardiac facility on our campus in La Jolla, among other major projects we are pursuing throughout our region. Best of all, we've solidified our reputation as a marquee employer, recognized year after year by *Fortune*, *Working Mother*, *AARP*, and other national news sources as one of America's "Best Places to Work."

People congratulate me on my success and ask how I did it. I tell them I didn't do anything; the people around me have made me successful—first and foremost, our front-line staff. All I do as a leader is take care of our people so they can provide superior care for our patients. Our leadership team spends time regularly with clerks, secretaries, doctors, nurses, IT technicians, environmental services personnel, front-line managers, parking lot attendants, and others, listening to their concerns and bonding with them on a personal level. It may sound unbelievable, but I respond to every single employee email I receive, often within minutes. I get out in the trenches to resolve staff issues through dialogue and the exchange of information rather than by dictating a solution from on high. At Scripps, we use systems that push authority, responsibility, and accountability as far down the chain of command as possible. All this amounts to a comprehensive, "front-line" approach to leadership, one that extends to every action our leadership team takes.

When our team makes a decision—whether it's about access to capital, investment in new technology, organizational change, the hiring of executives, or anything else—the first thing we consider is the implications for front-line staff. Likewise, and perhaps most important, we have made a public commitment to use layoffs as a last resort as opposed to a quick fix. This forces our leadership team to become more disciplined in our planning, so that we can ensure that we have the financial resources required to retain our employees, as well as systems in place to use employees effectively as our business changes. It forces us to become more innovative, so that we can anticipate market trends and protect jobs.

It is easy to talk about connecting with front-line workers, but many executives I meet tell me they don't know how to bridge this divide in practice. Beyond lip service and rhetoric, executives at some companies still remain removed from those employees as well as from the managers who oversee staff performance. *The Front-Line Leader* seeks to change this by showing executives not only how critical it is to connect with line personnel but also, in practical terms, how we have done it. Organizations could become far more successful if executives only understood what it is to lead authentically from the ground up, and if they committed themselves, as we have, to that approach. If connecting with front-line workers could yield success for a large health care company, just imagine what leaders in less volatile and less regulated industries could accomplish.

You may wonder whether our intense focus on front-line workers is too rigid or narrow. Can it really be wise to avoid layoffs at all costs or to spend so much time listening to employees' daily concerns? It's true that focusing on front-line workers requires sacrifice; for instance, the time I spend with employees means less time with other senior executives or community leaders. Yet the sacrifice is worth it. Paying attention to workers isn't only helpful—it's essential. Engaging with front-line employees emotionally, intellectually, and financially produces incredible loyalty. This in turn improves the kinds of metrics important to any business: retention, employee satisfaction, productivity, quality. It's not rocket science. When you have employees who feel cared for, they tend to care more themselves for the organization that provides their paycheck.

Beyond the business benefits, front-line leadership is simply the right thing to do. Do you find yourself thinking that we leaders today are losing sight of our true purpose? Rather than take care of our people, we're taking care of ourselves and our investors. Surely leaders have an obligation to increase stockholder and customer value, but we also must accept a profound responsibility to our people and their families. This responsibility goes beyond simply providing a fair paycheck, to also include some promise of job security and a real future. People say that the traditional, paternalist employment covenant between companies and employees is dead and buried, and with it the guarantee of a lifelong career at one employer. Maybe so, but we would do well on many levels to recover at least some of the moral sensibility that has made American industry the world's best.

You know, I never saw that CEO again after crossing paths with him in the basement. But if I could meet him today, I'd ask him if he liked his job. One of the greatest benefits of all in connecting with the front line is the significance it brings to the work of leadership. Sure, it's nice to turn around a failing organization, but it feels even better to see our people excited to do their jobs and willing to place their trust in our executives. Every day we're inspired to work even harder to earn their trust. Every day we feel that what we do has meaning.

We do need to work hard, because focusing intensely on front-line personnel isn't easy. It's a more challenging way to manage, requiring new levels of effort and thoughtfulness. If you're not willing to commit more of yourself over a period of years, this book is probably not for you. If you are willing, then give our approach a try. The following chapters are each organized around a principle and underlying tactics. Chapters One through Four cover basic practices of spending time with employees, communicating, and opening up psychologically. Chapters Five through Eight address corporate culture, covering concepts of advocacy and accountability as well as the culture-building role of middle managers. The final two chapters, Nine and Ten, suggest how strategy can be formed to support and benefit workers. Throughout, I draw on episodes from my career—especially my police experience, which strongly shaped how I view front-line interactions.

When it comes to the specific tactics, not everything I suggest will feel genuine or applicable to you. Industries and leaders are all different. Adapt the tactics to your circumstances and personality. Find your *own* authentic leadership style; your own unique way of listening to, helping, and engaging with your front line. Reconnect with any experiences you may have had working front-line jobs, and challenge the often formidable psychological distance between basement and boardroom. Your people will thank you, and so will your customers or patients. Your organization will gain new vitality that will ultimately translate to the bottom line.

Chapter One

Know Your People

I have this old, embarrassing photograph of myself wearing a Native American headdress. It's shoved into my desk drawer. Even though the corners are bent and I've got this big, silly grin on, the picture means as much to me as any of the framed images featuring famous people that line my office walls. The photograph dates from 1987, when I was vice president for support services at Anaheim Memorial Hospital in Anaheim, California. It was my first vice president job, and it put me in charge of an array of departments including environmental services (or housekeeping, as it was called back then), food services, engineering, and construction.

I made a practice at the time of meeting regularly with all of my staff, including the environmental service (EVS) workers. I'd go down to the EVS break room and say hello when employees were coming on duty and getting assignments for the shift. I wanted to know what my employees did; otherwise, I felt, I couldn't be an effective manager. I had learned as a police officer that if you wanted to get information about your beat, you had to be on the street talking to people. You had to develop rapport and trust, and after a while people would naturally start talking to you and telling you what they knew.

Sometimes I just sat and talked with the EVS staff; other times I went out and accompanied them on the job. They taught me how to use those big, circular floor polishers, and every time

I grasped the metal handles I was bucked around, much to their amusement. I didn't mind making myself a little vulnerable. Given how hesitant the employees acted around me and also how happy they seemed to see me, I surmised that I was probably among the few people from senior management to ever pay sincere attention to them.

As time passed, we built a relationship. The staff invited me to potlucks and other gatherings. "My boss's boss's boss knows more about what I do than my boss does," they would joke. They also challenged me to see if I could find dirt after they cleaned. "You guys are so good," I said, "I bet I can't find any." But I would still put on white gloves and poke around. A couple of times, to be honest, I did find a little bit of dirt on the gloves, but I never let them know. The point of this exercise was not for me to evaluate their performance. It was about going out there, showing I cared, and thanking the team for its hard work.

One day, a couple of the workers knocked on my door and asked me to accompany them to the break room. When we arrived, I found that all the employees had gathered. With smiles on their faces, they presented me with a Native American–style headdress they had made out of fur. It had two pointy horns protruding out of the top, a blue and red beaded design running across the front, and fluffy white feathers streaming down each side.

I held it in my hands and admired it. "This . . . is very nice. What is it?"

"This is for you," they said proudly. "Our chief."

Everyone applauded, and I didn't know what to say. What an incredible honor. Today, in addition to keeping that photograph in my drawer, I display the headdress in my office as a reminder of what I learned: that you can't be a distant boss and hope to be effective as a leader. You have to *connect* with people. You have to put time and energy into getting to know them and their work. Not just once. Or twice. Or three times. But regularly, month after month.

Fly-Bys Don't Count

Advice like this may sound familiar, but most CEOs and senior leaders don't do the kind of deep outreach I'm describing. More commonly they do what I call "fly-bys"; they flit in and out in a cursory manner—looking the part of the political candidate, shaking hands and kissing babies—not really bothering to *truly* engage with workers. Maybe they feel uncomfortable around line staff. Maybe they feel they have more important things to do. Maybe they're overwhelmed by the sheer size of their organization. Whatever the case, I doubt their attempts at outreach are doing as much good as they might think.

Here's an example. I once hired a chief nurse whom I'll call Marsha for one of our hospitals. Marsha's job was to oversee all nursing operations at her facility. Unfortunately, she became occupied with outside obligations, paying insufficient attention to her core duties. This led in short order to low morale among her workforce. Things got so bad that she had to leave the organization. Shortly after her departure, I happened to be in her hospital visiting my sick father-in-law. One of the nurses caring for him asked me to accompany her into the hallway for a private chat. "Chris," she said to me, "I wanted to thank you. I'm glad Marsha is no longer working with us."

"Why? You didn't like her?"

"No, because she was never here. Every so often she would throw on some scrubs so it would *look* like she was one of us. She would come up here and sweep through the units and smile and kind of talk to everyone a little bit. Then she'd disappear for months and you'd never see her. It was never real. We're glad she's gone."

Employees aren't stupid. They know a fly-by when they see it. By satisfying herself with fly-bys, Marsha was highlighting for her staff how *little* she cared about them. She wasn't bothering to listen, talk, and build relationships. She wasn't engendering trust. She was pretending to be one of the team—and, I would add, pretending to be a leader too.

Roll Up Your Sleeves and Get Dirty

In reaching out to employees, don't content yourself with just making conversation. Observe them on the job, actually serving customers. As an exercise, we regularly have groups of middle managers sit in our lobbies for an hour or more. Their mission is to watch the interactions between our volunteers, our staff, and our patients. Every time we do this, our managers return with valuable new perspectives. One HR manager sat in a hospital lobby that she normally walks through nine or ten times a day. Afterward, she bubbled over with ideas for improvement. "I don't want to badmouth my hospital, but I never realized how dark the lobby was! I also watched a volunteer at the registration desk who was trying to multitask, answering phone calls at the same time she was trying to give directions to patients. It was very disorganized. And employees were spending more time paying attention to their BlackBerries than to patients."

An even deeper way to get immersed is to pull up your sleeves and work with line employees yourself. When Hubert Joly took over as CEO of Best Buy in 2012, it was reported that one of the first things he planned to do was clock in at one of the company's retail locations to work the floor for the better part of a week. Noting that he hadn't clerked in a store for almost forty years, Joly related that he didn't want to learn about Best Buy "from the headquarters" but "from the front line."[1] This gesture must have helped Joly build relationships with his front-line personnel. It likely humanized him in their eyes, reinforcing the idea that he was just another Best Buy employee like them. Similarly, by letting myself get spun around by that floor polisher, I was acknowledging that I was no better or higher up than my workforce.

I don't know if Joly made these visits a regular feature of his tenure; I hope so, because working with the front line really makes an impact when it's done repeatedly. Our leadership team joins line workers at Scripps in a number of capacities, and it has become essential to our success. Once a year, for instance, as part of my ongoing training as an emergency medical technician, I trade in my suit for some scrubs and work in one of our emergency rooms as a technical partner. In a hospital, a technical partner works for and assists the nursing team; he's the person making and cleaning the beds, getting supplies, doing EKGs, taking blood pressures, and the like. During my shift, I'll tell the nurses not to treat me as the CEO, but as their trainee and subordinate. "I'm working for you," I'll say, "because you know more than I do about the work I'm doing today. So please guide me and help me to help you!"

And make no mistake, my gesture is not a put-on. It's real. Once, on my shift, a trauma came in, and the nurses had me throw on a lead protective apron (required during X-rays) and go up to the heliport with a nurse to accept a critical patient from the flight crew. Back in the trauma room, the surgeon had me stand right next to him. "Okay," he said, "you're going to help me deliver care. The patient has bilateral fractures from a motorcycle accident." And there I was, assisting the surgeon and nurses until the patient went to surgery. Although any assistance I provided was very limited and took place only under their complete guidance, I still soaked in the complexity of what the other caregivers were doing as well as the compassion with which they were delivering care. These professionals probably didn't have the knowledge or experience to run the whole health care system, but I couldn't do their jobs either. We had a lot to learn from each other. This meant that I needed to consult with them on decisions, not just assume I knew best because I had the "top job."

Obviously it's not possible to try everybody's job in your organization. But no matter what industry you're in or the size of your business, there are many ways to get a regular array of front-line experiences. One of my favorites is volunteering. I like to get out of the boardroom to teach first-aid classes to our front-line, nonclinical staff. This not only gives me another perspective on health care delivery but also allows me to engage with staff in an entirely different way. When I'm teaching, I'm no longer the CEO; I'm just another first-aid instructor.

For over a decade now, I have volunteered several times a month with the San Diego County Sheriff's Department Search and Rescue team; I hold the rank of Reserve Assistant Sheriff and am responsible for search and rescue and law enforcement reserves. The assignment gets me outdoors—hiking, rappelling, and driving around in the backcountry on 4x4s. The work is sobering, though; we search isolated, rural areas for people lost or stranded and in need of help, and we also perform searches for dead bodies and crime-related evidence. On one occasion, my team was out in the wilderness doing an event to raise awareness about search and rescue. Toward the end of the day, a young woman riding her horse past the event lost control. After hanging on for a quarter of a mile, she fell off, sustaining moderate injuries. I chased her down in one of our rescue vehicles and, along with some colleagues, provided first responder care. Afterward we placed her on a backboard and readied her for transport to the hospital.

I followed the ambulance to Scripps La Jolla and went inside, still wearing my sheriff's department uniform. The nurses on duty looked at me funny—they knew me, because this was the hospital where I did my EMT training, and they were not used to seeing me in this uniform. I asked how the injured woman was doing, and they told me she was fine and in a nearby room with her mother. I went to visit her and introduced myself. Her mother was surprised to learn that the CEO had been directly caring for her daughter. That meant a lot to her. And, as our chief medical officer has told me, my work in the field means a lot to our staff too.

I'm lucky to have a wife who gives me leeway during my off hours to volunteer like this. Rosemary herself volunteers on the front line, which further helps me build a strong relationship with our workforce. Rosemary loves dogs, and she enjoys bringing our Labrador retriever into Scripps facilities for pet therapy visits. Certified therapy dogs like our Amber help alleviate stress and even pain for patients and staff. In her presence, patients feel connected to their homes and their own pets, and they're distracted for a moment from being in a hospital.

Rosemary visits with Amber as often as she can, sometimes a couple of times a week, so she's a familiar sight around Scripps. She doesn't announce that she's my wife, but when someone recognizes her, she'll confirm that she's married to me. Thanks to these little moments, people seem to understand that I'm not just "the CEO" but a regular guy with a wife and a dog. From that, they feel that much better about their own jobs and the organization for which they work.

To be clear, I don't volunteer on search and rescue or as a first-aid instructor specifically seeking to make an impression on front-line personnel and patients. If that were the case, my efforts would probably appear contrived. I volunteer because as a former police officer, I feel fulfilled protecting people and rendering assistance in their time of need. If you're a manager or executive and you're interested in having more of a presence on the front line, find something you're passionate about and volunteer for its own sake. The benefits of staying close to line employees will emerge in due course, without your having to make a special effort. You'll be surprised how enjoyable you'll find it and how much it helps you as a leader.

Do Your Dance

It can be difficult to attribute a clear, quantitative business benefit to time spent on the front line or to any other tactic presented in this book; determining causality is just too complicated. The incredible financial and operational results we've seen at Scripps have resulted from many tactics *working together* over a period of years. Yet the physical presence of a leader is powerful—I know, because I've seen its effects firsthand.

In 1997, I left a position as CEO of Anaheim Memorial Hospital, a 240-bed facility, and took over as CEO of Long Beach

Memorial Medical Center, a much larger, 700-bed facility. The Medical Center had a long central corridor that stretched from the Children's Hospital to the Women's Hospital all the way to the Rehabilitation Hospital and an attached skilled nursing facility. This corridor was so big that at any given time you might see hundreds of employees walking from place to place. What I noticed immediately upon joining Long Beach Memorial was that very few of the employees said hello to one another. They were all rushing, paying little attention. It was a huge difference from Anaheim Memorial, where everyone greeted each other by name.

Witnessing people walk right past one another made me uncomfortable, so I decided, in a small way, to do something about it. I began walking that corridor and saying hello to as many people as I could. This wasn't easy at first: because I was the new CEO, many people didn't recognize me. And because they walked with their heads down, staring at the floor, I literally had to duck down in order to make eye contact and say, "Hey there! How are you?"

I kept doing this, month after month. I also used these walks to rub scuff marks off the floor with my leather-bottomed shoe. After about a year, I began to notice a change. People were looking up more, even saying hello to me. More important, they were saying hello to one another. The whole atmosphere became friendlier. People began to joke about my habit of rubbing off scuff marks, calling my particular style of walking the "CEO walk." Eventually one of my managers dubbed it the "Van Gorder dance." Other employees and managers started doing the dance (which incidentally resulted in noticeably cleaner floors). The entire culture of this relatively large organization began to shift, perhaps in part because their leader had left the boardroom and was regularly engaging with the workforce.

Of course, there was more to that story. In a large organization, cultural change occurs only if *everyone* in a supervisory capacity walks the hallways and does their own versions of the

Van Gorder dance. At Scripps, we now hold managers formally accountable for making rounds with their employees. It's part of their performance evaluation; if they don't do enough rounding, they miss out on some incentive compensation. This sends a message to managers, one that I hope you will heed as well. Face time with employees is something you *need* to do, not an option you might entertain. It's critical to the success of any team, department, or organization.

Make It Real with Questions and Answers

Make no mistake: rounding alone won't cut it. With almost fourteen thousand employees under my watch, our leadership team can't regularly interact with each one or even a majority of them on a one-on-one basis. Fortunately, we've developed other communications tactics that allow us to remain meaningfully accessible on a broader scale to line employees and managers. These tactics allow us to keep tabs on what's going on in our workplaces, *and* they reinforce the notion that we're leaders who genuinely care.

First, we hold transparent question-and-answer sessions with groups of line employees and managers. I started doing informational meetings early on in my career when I was head of security and safety at Los Angeles' Orthopaedic Hospital. Every so often, without thinking much about it, I would gather the troops and simply tell them what was going on throughout the organization. I was willing to talk about anything, so long as it wasn't confidential. After a year, I noticed that none of our security officers were leaving the company. This was highly unusual; in most industries security officers didn't get paid much and turnover was high.

"It's surprising," I said to a couple of the department supervisors one day. "We've had the same staff now for a couple of years. Nobody is leaving for other jobs. What's going on?"

They told me that the department felt loyal simply because I spent time talking to them; it meant as much to them as their paycheck. Because most other managers didn't openly share information with their teams, our staff had become information sources for the entire organization. Even some of the doctors had taken to asking the security officers for updates.

That was a wake-up call. I realized that the higher up you get in an organization, the more vital it is that you serve as a teacher and communicator. Today I make sure to get out on a weekly basis to talk to groups and answer their questions. I might arrive at a hospital break room and invite employees to come and chat. To show respect for the chain of command, I always call ahead, letting managers on site know I'm coming and asking them to participate in the session with me. The last thing I want is managers thinking that I've come to spy on them.

When I lead these gatherings, I make sure not to deliver a lecture, opting instead for Q&A sessions. I want the staff to know I'm comfortable with tough questioning, as it gives me the opportunity to teach. I have a rule that *anything* is a valid topic of discussion, with only three exceptions: I won't violate patient confidentiality, I won't discuss personnel issues relating to specific individuals, and I won't discuss business arrangements that have confidentiality agreements. Within these constraints, I tell employees to have at it.

Much of the time employees don't ask tough, probing questions; they don't feel the need to test me, because they've come to know over time that they have both my attention and my commitment to give them real answers. Sometimes they do push the envelope, though. On one occasion, physicians at one of our hospitals were furious that we had acquired a competing medical group. The medical group had been on the verge of bankruptcy, and the doctors at our hospital saw this group as rivals. Why should money our doctors had brought into the system be used to bail out their competitors? I held a Q&A session, and some of the physicians got up and told me, "We're angry. Remember how we voted 'no confidence' in your predecessor? We can do it with you too."

I explained the decision and rationale to them in detail—with facts and figures. "Look," I told them, "give me some time, and let me see if we can turn the medical group around and make it profitable. As we go along, I will give you updates and show you the numbers." And that's what I did. The medical group's performance improved dramatically during the next couple of years, and as I promised, I continued to hold sessions with the physicians to keep them informed. About two years later, a physician at one of the sessions began to harangue me again about the purchase of the group. To my surprise and pleasure, another physician stood up. "Guys, stop it. Enough is enough. Chris has done everything he promised. He has turned the medical group around, and he has been forthright. It's time for us to get off his back."

The whole room went silent. For several years before then, Scripps had been plagued by conflict between administrators and the physicians who work at our hospitals. It meant something that a physician was now publicly jumping onto our side over a very sensitive matter. Afterward, this issue lost its emotional intensity. We were able to come together, thanks in part to the years of work our leadership team had put in getting to know the physicians and communicating transparently with them to address their concerns.

Stay Accessible

When I meet with groups of employees, physicians, and managers, I always conclude by telling them if they ever have a problem they can't resolve, they should feel free to email me directly anytime. I encourage them to operate within the chain of command, but if for some reason that fails, they have the right to contact me. And as employees are surprised to discover, they will always get a prompt response. That's because, again, I make a practice of responding to every single employee email, usually the same day and most of the time within minutes.

I've been responding to all employee emails since the early 1990s, when email first appeared. Before then, business was conducted mainly over the phone, and I believed that if someone phoned me, I should return the call as soon as possible. What frustrated me about phone calls were the endless, time-consuming bouts of phone tag that would arise. Email by comparison seemed incredibly efficient. You could skim an email to get to the key point. It took only a few seconds to hit Reply and get back to someone. You could respond at a time convenient for you and avoid playing phone tag. I got in the habit of making sure I never left work without handling every email in my inbox.

Today I keep my BlackBerry with me wherever I go (set on vibrate!). If I'm at home reading or watching a football game, I'll feel it go off and answer it immediately. If I'm at work and not in a meeting, I'll also dash off a few lines and press Send. I can do this extremely quickly (more quickly than ever, since a transcription program on my phone lets me talk out my emails), and I can also quickly distinguish between messages that need a response and junk messages that don't.

I regard email as a core part of my job, a digital form of the in-person rounding that all leaders need to do. Email allows me to keep current on what employees are thinking about the organization, their bosses, and my own performance. Sometimes the information I get is positive, sometimes not, but either way I have a chance to teach by explaining issues that arise. I get to do this teaching in a customized way instead of writing a generic memo, hoping it covers the topic. And employees really appreciate that. I can't tell you how many people have emailed me saying, "Wow, I can't believe how fast you responded," or "I can't believe you responded at all!" I've even been able to intervene in many misunderstandings and get them resolved before they blew out of control.

Email has also allowed me to build personal connections with individuals I wouldn't have been able to meet in person. I have line employees who have emailed just to see if I really would respond and who have kept checking in regularly with me, keeping me updated on developments in their careers and personal lives. Everybody knows that if they communicate with me, they're *going* to hear back. This flattens the organization, breaking down the notion of the executive suite as an impenetrable ivory tower. Besides, emailing with employees is fun. Sure, I get messages from people who have a problem and are angry. But I get many more from people who love their work, love Scripps, and just want to let me know.

Keeping Employees Current

Another critically important way I keep in touch in the digital age is through something I call "Market News." Every day, seven days a week, I get up early and search the media for relevant articles to send to Scripps managers, physicians, and employees. These articles cover medical developments as well as technological, political, and economic trends that affect our industry. I summarize these articles in an email and send it out to hundreds of people. I'm an avid photographer, so I always drop in a couple of nice shots I have taken or that front-line employees have shared with me. Some employees may just glance at the pictures and proceed with their work, but that's okay; at least they're opening the email and possibly scanning the news headlines, occasionally diving into a topic of interest. In some small way I'm able to make a daily connection with them that I might not otherwise have made.

One of the greatest things about Market News is that it allows me to give Scripps employees an understanding of the big-picture context affecting the health care industry and to do it a little bit each day so that it's manageable. Market News reminds me of the neighborhood watch meetings I used to run as a police officer. At neighborhood watch, citizens can get a broader picture of what's going on in their city or state, and they can connect that picture with what they see happening in their local neighborhoods. Neighborhood watch meetings also invite dialogue—as does Market News. Every day employees email me about items they've found interesting, asking specific questions and giving me still more opportunities to teach.

Employees who like Market News also occasionally email asking what service I use to produce it. "It's not a service," I reply. "*I'm* the service." There are two reasons I feel compelled to do Market News myself. First, it's a good discipline for me, because I need to keep up on industry news myself if I'm going to make informed strategic decisions. More important, I don't want my employees and managers staying up to date by reading things some other service thinks they should be reading. I want them reading news that *I* think is important.

As I've mentioned, we have a no-layoff philosophy at Scripps—a key part of my front-line approach to leadership. But how can employees at Scripps come to appreciate how special that is if they aren't aware of all the ugly layoffs that have been occurring throughout our industry? Among the many dozens of articles I cover each week, I make sure to include some that report on layoffs in our region and elsewhere. When bad news happens at Scripps, as it inevitably will, I'll also include reports on that. On a few occasions, a Scripps facility was unfortunately listed on a California state government list of hospitals that have been fined for a violation. When that happened, I put articles announcing it in Market News, just as I insert similar information about other health care organizations. It's important for employees to feel they're getting the honest truth, not just the good news about Scripps.

Be Yourself

Interacting personally with employees isn't just about you getting to know them; it's also about them getting to know you in a transparent way. And not just your beliefs or your positions on burning business issues, but also your experiences, your personality, who you are, and what you're made of. I became aware of this during a Q&A session I held in 2013 at Scripps Mercy Hospital. I went in prepared to talk about the usual items: the state of Scripps finances, recent decisions we've made, the Affordable Care Act and how that might affect us going forward, and so on. When the session started, I was greeted, as I often am, by a brief period of shy silence as employees considered what questions to ask. Finally the manager in the room said, "You know what they want to know, Chris? They want to know who *you* are."

This pushed me a little off balance. "Okay," I responded. "What in particular do you want to know about?"

"Well, tell them how you got this job and the fact that you used to be a policeman and a security guard and all that."

So that's what I did. I spent a half hour telling my story. I thought about stopping, but every time I did, I saw from their faces that the employees were truly interested. Afterward, individuals came up to me and sent me emails thanking me for telling them about who I was. What they wanted, I think, was to know that their leader, and by implication their organization, had a moral compass. They also wanted to know that I was a human being, someone to whom they could relate. I in turn wanted to let them know I had once been a clerk in the emergency room and I had worked my way up; I wanted to convey that it was possible for *every single one of them* to accomplish something similar if they so desired and were willing to put in the effort.

I'm not advising that you write an autobiography or that you spend hours talking about yourself wherever you go. Just speak honestly about your background when people ask. Even if you never held a front-line position in your life, you certainly will have something in your past—some challenge, some personal struggle—with which line employees can connect. And in everything you do, try to have fun and let your personality shine through. During each of the last few years, I've done a cameo in a spoof video to promote a movie event we offer our employees.

In past videos, I've dressed up as Commander James T. Kirk from *Star Trek* and as an agent from *Men in Black*. At another event, called Scripps Night at the Ballpark, I greet thousands of our employees and shake their hands as they push through the entrance at a San Diego Padres game. Make yourself accessible. Be visible. And do it in a way that feels natural.

The Job Never Ends

Rounding, volunteering on the front lines, running question-and-answer sessions, answering employee emails, participating in videos—all this may sound like a tall order, even downright exhausting. It is a lot of work. I estimate I spend at least 25 percent of my time getting physically in front of my line employees and managers, and up to 50 percent of my time communicating or teaching in some capacity. I do it because I want to build trusting relationships with our line employees, no matter where in the organization they happen to be. I want to know about the realities of our work environments so I can make good administrative decisions. I want to educate and spread information, so baseless and destructive rumors don't have a chance to take hold.

Getting to know your people means engaging all the way. I sometimes talk to groups of college kids, and the first question they ask is, "How much money do you make?" I always respond, "More money than I ever thought I would." Their next question: "Tell me what your typical day is like." I tell them there is no typical day. But then I go off and relate how I work late into the evening, answering emails and responding to anything that might come up. Watching the eyes of these young people, I can see them thinking, *Yeah, I want to make the money, but I don't really want to do all that work.*

I don't blame them. I've accepted a calling to be a leader. Staying truly engaged with our entire organization means being available 24/7, even when I'm on vacation. That's the sacrifice required. But the blessings far outweigh the sacrifice. Remaining connected with street-level realities is a labor of love for me, just as it was when I was a cop. In fact, despite all I already do to get to know my people, I wish I could do more. People sometimes greet me in the hallway at a Scripps facility and say, "Oh, wow, Mr. Van Gorder. I've only seen you in photographs." I apologize, telling them, "I'm sorry, it's such a big organization. I wish I could know you personally." And that's the truth. I really do.

Taking Action

To know your people better:

- Invest time and energy in personal engagement, to truly lead at every level of an organization.
- Make drop-ins regular and genuine, with substantive interactions. Employees know a fly-by when they see it.
- Use Q&A sessions, emails, and other regular communications to stay in touch with large groups of employees.
- Open up about yourself; let employees know the real you. You'll find they respect and trust you even more.

Chapter Two

Get Outside Yourself

On October 17, 1978, when I was working as a street cop in Monterey Park, California, I responded to a domestic dispute, which can be one of the most dangerous calls an officer receives. A distraught woman had seized her infant child from her estranged husband, barricaded herself in her car, and refused to give the child back. The woman warned her husband not to call the police, claiming she would "ram" any police car that showed up.

Spotting the woman and her husband, I stepped out of my patrol car and approached. The woman, seeing a second police car pull up, fled the scene, her crying baby strapped in a car seat. I ran back to my vehicle and ordered the other officer to pursue the woman. Jamming my car into gear, I turned onto a nearby cross street, hoping to intercept the woman at the next block. I took a right onto the street parallel to the one I'd been on, only to find this woman's car heading straight for me, now with two police cars in hot pursuit. That's the last thing I remember. Witnesses saw the suspect accelerate and crash head-on into my patrol car. The impact sent my car bucking into the air and careening backward ten to fifteen feet. My body first slammed against the steering wheel, my bulletproof vest cushioning the blow. Then, despite the seatbelt I was wearing, I flew briefly into the air and my skull banged against the roof.

When I regained consciousness a few seconds later, my neck felt numb. I tried to get out of the car, but my body wouldn't move as it was supposed to. My fellow officers rushed over to help me. The car was totaled, and it took some time for them to safely extract me. Emergency medical services stabilized me and took me to a local community hospital, where I received emergency care and was admitted. A few days later, I was transferred to another hospital, Los Angeles Orthopaedic, where the doctors told me I had sustained serious damage to my spine at my neck and lower back. They considered performing a risky surgery but decided against it in favor of intensive traction and physical therapy. "You will likely have issues for the rest of your life," they said when I was discharged, "but give it time. With hard work, your body will start to heal on its own."

That has been the case. But in the short term, my body was as wrecked as my patrol car. It was hard for me to move—I felt numbness and weakness in my limbs as well as crushing pain in my head. Going back to work was out of the question; I had to take high doses of painkillers just to get through the day.

After a year of demanding physical therapy and additional hospital admissions, I had improved somewhat, but remained in constant pain. Our department chief offered me a choice: take a light-duty assignment or accept early retirement. Unable to stomach the idea of a boring desk job, I chose retirement, an option that initially didn't work out well. I had been a cop for a relatively short period of time, but I had loved every minute of it and was living my dream. Now I didn't know what to do with myself. Depressed and angry, I sat around all day watching TV and eating, packing on seventy-five pounds. Things got so bad I visited a psychiatrist, who proclaimed me "borderline suicidal" and wrote me a prescription for antidepressants.

That was the wakeup call I needed. I couldn't continue feeling sorry for myself; I had to move on. The next day, I tossed out the prescription, threw on my sneakers, gritted my teeth, and challenged myself to go for a run—frankly, more of a walk—despite the pain. I made it a few hundred yards before I had to stop. The day after that, I managed a few hundred yards again. The day after that, I went farther—a quarter mile. Then I made it a half-mile. Then a mile. As the weeks passed, the pounds melted off and I felt better. I also got a start in a new career, interviewing for a job managing security for Los Angeles Orthopaedic Hospital, the same hospital that had provided most of my care. Although I had been a security officer before, I had no experience running an entire operation. Still, the job was open, and I thought I could do a good job. I convinced management to hire me by pledging to work at minimum wage for ninety days.

"Just give me a chance to prove myself," I pleaded. "You won't be disappointed." Management gave me that chance, and the rest, as they say, is history.

I often think back to this challenging time when I *wasn't* the "big boss." Staying physically close to employees is important, but to reap the full benefits of front-line leadership, you need to internalize the connection and make a practice of staying *psychologically* close as well. One of the greatest problems leaders face is the distancing that can take place in their own minds when they lose perspective and start to think of themselves primarily in terms of their titles. In my case, it helps me to remember that I once lost everything, was "borderline suicidal," and had to plead for a chance to start anew. Putting my identity as an executive into perspective, I am better able to see myself in our front-line workers and our front-line workers in me. The higher you move up the ladder, the more work and vigilance it takes to remember your roots—but leading from the front line requires nothing less.

See Yourself as a Trainee Again

Perhaps you didn't start at the bottom or experience a career transition. What else can you do to adjust your thinking so you can form authentic emotional connections with others? Easy: make a regular practice of remembering those times when you screwed up and learned something new. Most executives I speak to can think of at least one or two spectacular flameouts they've survived. I know I can.

One night when I was a cop, I was on patrol when I observed a motorcycle blow through a red light at high speed. I activated my emergency lights and pulled the motorcyclist over. As the guy was coming to a stop, his cycle hit the curb and he fell off his bike. *Okay*, I thought, *this guy is drunk*. I needed to do a field sobriety test, so I followed our standard protocol and called for backup. When another officer arrived, I asked the suspect to lean against my car and I patted him down for weapons. I started at his neck and continued through his torso, around his midsection and around each leg. The man turned out to be cooperative, respect-ful, and a generally nice guy. "Hey, officer," he said to me as I did my work, "I know I've been drinking. I'm really sorry. That was stupid of me. I think I'm flat-out drunk."

He continued to chat me up as I performed sobriety tests, hav-ing him balance on one foot, touch the tip of his nose with his eyes closed and so on. "You know," he said, "I like cops. I really appreciate the things you guys do every day to keep us safe." The other officer and I laughed—most people we pulled over for drunk driving didn't thank us for our service.

I completed the tests, and the guy failed miserably. *What a shame*, I thought, that a guy like this had screwed up. As I pulled out my handcuffs, the man said, "Boy, I'm sorry. I shouldn't have done this. I know I'm going to jail." He belched and blinked a few times. "Hey, I just thought of something. Do you want my gun?"

What!?

I instinctively moved away from the man. The other offi-cer, standing nearby, swiveled and placed his hand over his weapon, ready to cover me in case anything happened.

The motorcyclist nodded. "Yeah, I've got a gun in my boot. You missed it when you did the pat down."

Checking the man's boot, I found that sure enough, he had a small revolver hidden deep inside it. Confiscating the gun, I had to arrest him for both carrying a concealed weapon and drunk driving. As we drove the man to the station, I felt sick to my stomach. I should've found that gun. I had totally, utterly screwed up, putting my life at risk as well as my fellow officer's. How had that happened? I knew how to do a proper search. But obviously I hadn't been thorough enough.

I was an experienced officer, but that mistake made me feel like a rookie all over again. I became far more diligent in every pat down I performed—and that was a good thing. Today, I continue to feel like a rookie all over again by reliving the episode in my mind. When I find myself becoming a little too smug as a CEO, I alert myself to all the ways that I'm still learning. This leaves me feeling that much closer to that young nurse and that information technologist who are also feeling their way ahead.

Engage Even More Deeply

Another way to stay psychologically close to workers is to be mindful of how you engage and interact with them. There are ways to structure your time on the front line that enable you not only to build relationships but also to *empathize* with a worker's experience.

I've mentioned that when I work in the emergency room each year, I put myself under the charge of the line employees there. Likewise, when I volunteer on the search and rescue team, I technically work for a sergeant in the sheriff's department. He is the boss, and I am his employee. In fact, I call him "boss" in my emails to him, and every year he gives me a formal performance evaluation. In such interactions, the message I'm implicitly affirming to myself is: *I, Chris Van Gorder, may be a CEO, but that doesn't mean other people aren't more qualified than me in some areas. My title goes only so far.*

It may sound strange for an executive to enjoy having others act as his boss. I've spent my career building authority—why give that up? I have three answers. First, in temporarily relinquishing authority, you get back *more* of it. That's because workers bestow informal respect on you along with their loyalty. Second, I admit it: I'm a strange CEO. But at least I'm not (I hope) an arrogant, entitled, or distanced CEO, which would be far worse. Finally, I must confess that briefly identifying as a line employee can come as a bit of a relief. It's nice sometimes to not have to shoulder all the responsibility that comes with being the CEO. When I'm volunteering, out there on the trail with my twenty-pound pack, I can relax and focus on the work at hand, which is enjoyable in and of itself. It's a great way to rebalance my life.

To empathize even more with workers during front-line experiences, focus intently on listening. As a police officer, I was trained to become situationally aware—to scrutinize my surroundings and come to rapid judgments during dangerous or emergency situations. We would be driving along in a patrol car, and my training officer would abruptly turn to me and say, "Chris, where are we?"

"What?"

"Where are we *right now?* What address?"

I would start to look around for the address.

He would shake his head. "Uh-uh, Chris, there's no time for that. You need to know your surroundings at all times. If shots are fired and you're requesting help, you need to tell the dispatcher where to send backup, and you have to do it *fast.*"

In the business world, being situationally aware involves staying attuned to subtler dimensions of communication, like tone of voice or facial gestures. It's about getting an intuitive feel for how workers and managers walk as you pass them in the hallway or how they greet you. What's morale like? Are people happy?

Depressed? Anxious? Upset? Situational awareness directs your attention away from yourself and all that *you* are. Your executive ego seems to evaporate as you put yourself *right there* with others, empathizing with their concerns. Conversely, it's hard to be situationally aware when you're fixated on your own prestige or accomplishments. You can become utterly blind to what's going on around you.

In cultivating situational awareness, you start to notice all kinds of interesting things about your organization. And you notice wonderful people, too, individuals who carry their own messages of attentiveness and service. At Scripps, we have a parking attendant whom people refer to as the "Thank You Man." Babajan is an immigrant from Iran who left his entire family behind as he went in search of opportunity. When he first arrived in the United States, he got a job in an ice cream store and taught himself English. While scooping ice cream, he learned that saying "Thank you" to people got them to smile and engage with him. Later, at Scripps, he started saying "Thank you" to people he met, acknowledging them for everything and anything: "Thank you for wearing that wonderful new suit today"; "Thank you for smiling"; "Thank you for thanking me"; "Thank you for thanking me for thanking you"—and so on. By taking every opportunity to express gratitude, Babajan gets patients at our hospital to smile, even those who may have received bad news about their health. He reminds me every day to get outside myself, appreciate the way others are behaving, and express my gratitude.

Lean on Your Partners

I'm fortunate to have many people around me on whom I can lean in order to escape my executive identity and stay grounded. An important tactic, in fact, is to *deliberately* cultivate partners at home and at work that see past your title and enable you to do so as well. In my case, there's my wife, Rosemary, whom I met long before I ever became a senior leader. Every year at Scripps Night at the Ballpark, the same family comes up and asks to have their pic-ture taken with me. Rosemary sees this and laughs. At some point in the evening, she pulls me aside and says, "Chris, who would ever believe that people would want to have their pictures taken with *you*?" Thanks to Rosemary, I'm able to laugh at myself. I'm really not an executive at my core. Not to mention, the moment I get home, I stop being CEO because we both know *she's* the CEO in our family.

Colleagues at Scripps also help me stay psychologically close to our workers. You hear a lot from CEOs about how lonely it is at the top. I don't feel lonely, because I have purposely surrounded myself with a group of confidants whom I trust to puncture the "CEO bubble." Although most of these individuals report formally to me, they are also loyal friends and as such are willing to give me honest and sometimes tough feedback about my performance. Their unusual frankness improves my own decision making while also bringing me back down to earth and reminding me of my true identity and purpose as a leader.

One of my confidants, Elliot Kushell, isn't an employee, which allows for even more pointed feedback. Although I hired Elliot as a consultant to handle organizational development work for Scripps, he also serves as a close advisor and coach. Facilitating our senior management retreats, he makes sure everyone's perspective gets heard, and he helps me correct myself in real time, allowing me to prevent minor errors from becoming major issues. When I am too forceful with a colleague or not forceful enough, or when I haven't given certain factors enough weight in my decision-making process, Elliot lets me know.

Like situational awareness, my reliance on close confidants has its origins in my time as a cop. Sitting together in our patrol car for eight hours or more at a stretch, my partner and I devel-oped an emotionally close relationship, talking and joking about everything, even topics we wouldn't discuss with our loved ones.

It went without saying that if either of us was ever tempted to let the powers of being a police officer go to our heads, the other was there to set him straight.

When I first arrived at Scripps, I wanted to see if I could recover this kind of closeness among my top executives, recognizing that I was their boss and not a peer. I began by deviating from the usual new CEO practice of replacing the existing leadership team. Our organization had been failing, but I didn't perceive that the executives in place were to blame, so I wound up keeping all but one. Rather than telling these leaders they needed to prove themselves to me, I made it known that I trusted them implicitly and that trust was theirs to lose. Building on this affirming message, I made it my mission to really get to know these people, while always making it clear that as their boss I would hold them accountable for their performance.

My leadership team coalesced very quickly. The honesty and friendship of these executives allowed me to open up with them when I faced difficult decisions or moments of doubt. Whereas many senior leaders feel compelled to always project an image of strength and confidence, I was able to approach members of my leadership team and say, "Look, I'm thinking of terminating somebody or moving the entire organization in a whole new direction, and before I make the public announcement that we're going to do this, what do you think? Am I totally off base?" The resulting conversations were a great reality check on my thought process.

That is not to say I am ever *completely* transparent about my fears and insecurities. Even today, almost fifteen years into my tenure at Scripps, I realize there is a balance to be struck. In a tough industry like ours, I need to keep morale up among top executives by playing cheerleader. On the whole, though, strong partner-style relationships do let me be myself. I don't get too hung up on the power differentials that exist between my leadership team, employees outside the executive suite, and myself.

If you already have close confidants you can rely on, be sure to constantly solicit feedback by asking questions. You may not like the answers you receive, but chances are you'll find them immensely valuable. On one occasion, I asked my team to identify the biggest item we don't usually discuss—the "elephant in the room" question. To my great surprise and discomfort, the team blurted out the name of a manager at Scripps—I'll call her Sally Smith.

"Who?" I asked.

"Sally Smith," they said. "She's the elephant in the room. We don't think you're managing her well. She's undermining you, and you're not doing a damn thing about it." They explained that Smith was subverting one of our major corporate initiatives; they offered me specific examples of problematic actions Smith had taken.

I had known Smith was struggling with our initiative, but I hadn't appreciated just how much.

"This is pretty staggering," I said, "but you're right; I haven't been managing Sally well." She had been with our organization a long time, and, as I further acknowledged to my team, I have a tendency to give long-term employees more rope—sometimes to my detriment. I asked my team to document their concerns, and I subsequently used the information they provided to deal with Smith and get her back on track. Had I not had my group of confidants giving me feedback, problems with Smith might have continued for years, and resentment would have built up among my team at the poor job I was doing managing her. Meanwhile, I would have gone about my business thinking I was doing my job.

Build a Team Early

Now is the time to start building a core team and to get in the habit of receiving honest feedback, especially if you're a young, ambitious manager. You'll make better decisions throughout your career, feel happier and more authentic on the job, and stay more connected to workers. On the other hand, if you wait too long and develop a reputation as an overly controlling leader, you'll have a harder time establishing a team of close confidants with whom to partner. Other senior executives won't believe you when you suddenly gather them around and say, "I want honest feedback." Fearing for their own jobs, they'll treat you solely as the CEO, not also as their trusted colleague.

Starting early means that by the time you become a senior leader, you have individuals on your team who have known you for years and who are thus able to keep you grounded. When we're meeting with workers and front-line managers, my longtime consultant Elliot (whom I've known since 1986) will often introduce me to the group by saying, "You know, I've known Chris ever since he was a young vice president. And he is the same person now as he was then." Hearing that statement coming from Elliot means a lot. Regardless of the statement's veracity, I always take it as a gentle reminder to not forget my roots. *Take pride in your accomplishments*, Elliot's telling me, *but see yourself as the person you really are*. Hearing this regularly has helped balance out the awards and accolades I've received and has minimized the chances that they'll go to my head.

In assembling your team, seek out potential partners who are able to stay grounded themselves. I tend to promote from within and hire people who used to work on the front lines; I find that such individuals tend to be more grateful for their jobs and mindful of their roots and their responsibilities to others. Our brilliant general counsel was initially a carpenter and went to law school only after his wife signed him up for the LSAT and urged him to take the exam. He wound up missing only three questions and was admitted to Boston University. Today he still goes home every day, puts aside his title, and cares for his family. He doesn't get carried away by what or who he has become, and he wouldn't tolerate it if I did either.

"We," Not "I"

One of the best and more rewarding ways to get outside yourself is to share the credit whenever possible. Speak in terms of "we," not "I." *We* lowered costs by 3 percent last year; *we* have successfully initiated a new procedure for reducing patient wait times and increasing satisfaction. By sharing the credit as much as possible (and by also being the first to accept blame when things don't go well), you invite others to stand with you on the pedestal the leader might otherwise occupy alone. If there's an ego trip to be had, let's *all* take it! As one of our medical researchers told me in an email, "When I think of leaders who have the respect of their team, they are the leaders who think in terms of 'we,' not 'me.'" Sharing the credit is also just truthful, because let's face it, no leader accomplishes anything by herself. Leaders may be more visible, but achievement always reflects a team effort, and everyone's contribution counts. The longer I serve as a leader, the more I realize that it's *those around me* who actually get things done; what I do is chart the course. As I tell Scripps employees, we will fail as an organization unless *everybody* does their jobs.

If that's the case, you might ask, how come I'm writing this book? Aren't *I* taking the credit for our organizational successes? I struggled mightily with this question, because that's absolutely *not* the message I want to convey. My goal here is simply to share some of the things I have learned as a result of my experiences as a leader. I have tried throughout to share credit and speak of "we" as much as possible, recognizing as well that the conventions of narrative prose require that I use "I" at times. Let me make a blanket declaration right now: *everyone* at Scripps is responsible for what we have accomplished. It's not me that deserves the credit. It's our employees, physicians, donors, volunteers, and board members.

More generally, it's so important for CEOs not to fall into the trap of believing that they, as the chief executive, are the corporation. To prevent that from happening, I engage in a little thought experiment every night as I drive home. I imagine what the founders of my organization, Ellen Browning Scripps and Mother Mary Michael Cummings, would think of the events, decisions, or accomplishments of the day. I share the results of this thought exercise with my employees as a way of both connecting us all to the greater legacy of our company and emphasizing that I know I am merely a steward of the company's legacy. In the same vein, our general counsel has at times reminded me that he is the company's lawyer, not *my* lawyer, and that he will be obligated to disagree with me on occasion. I don't see this as a challenge; rather, I have shared his reminder with other senior executives and groups of employees. Like the thought exercise with our founders, our general counsel's point serves to remind me and other employees that we are all part of the larger whole, and that we must not let our own individual egos get in the way.[1]

Love Your People

Psychological distance is extremely dangerous for leaders. When you lose perspective and start to think you're something more than just another member of the team, you undercut any progress you might have been making in building trust and affection between yourself and your workforce. Workers sense your egotism and arrogance and distance themselves. Small conflicts become bigger conflicts. Loyalty and job satisfaction plummet.

This is not to suggest that executives should dispense with their egos entirely, or that they shouldn't be proud of all they've accomplished. Leaders, by their very nature, tend to have strong egos—that's how we got where we are. We *should* be confident, and there are times on the job when we *need* to boldly invoke the prestige of our titles. Most other times, though, titles seem to get in the way. They inhibit the emotional connection that can make a leader more than just another boss—and by extension, an organization more than just another place to work. Lodged too deeply in a CEO's mind, they can nudge him away from his people, when he should be trying to draw closer.

The question arises: How close? Executives talk a lot about "passion" in connection with the workplace, but they seldom use the word "love." Maybe "love" sounds too soft or touchy-feely—not relevant for the uncompromising world of business. As an ex-cop, I'm here to say it is relevant. I love each and every member of my leadership team. I feel even *more* attached to our employees, in ways I can't fully articulate. I'm not ashamed to say I've gotten emotional when thinking about the prospect of being unable to preserve everyone's job in the event of a massive shift in the industry. That's in part because I used to be a line employee myself, but also because of tactics I apply every day to get me beyond my CEO identity. No matter what your training or background, you can love your people too. And the more emotionally attached you get to your workers, the more your workers will love and respect you. They'll see your interest in them as genuine—because it *will be*.

Taking Action

To get outside yourself:

- Practice reflecting on your mistakes and the lessons you have learned from them. Encourage your first reports to do the same.
- Put yourself in situations where front-line employees are serving as your boss or where you can at least work side by side with them.
- Cultivate situational awareness. Forget about yourself for a moment and pay closer attention to what others are saying and doing.
- Assemble a team of people around you who aren't cowed by your title. Encourage them to help you keep it real.
- Share the credit. You're not the entire corporation. Think and talk in terms of "we," not "I."

Chapter Three

The Credibility Factor

September 2005 is a month many Scripps employees won't soon forget. Hurricane Katrina had struck about two weeks earlier, devastating New Orleans and nearby areas. Thousands of survivors had been evacuated to the Houston, Texas, area to receive aid and temporary lodging. Most survivors who had experienced acute injuries had already been treated, but many others, suffering from chronic conditions like diabetes and mental health issues such as post-traumatic stress, still needed help. Responding to a request from then–United States Surgeon General Dr. Richard Carmona, Scripps dispatched a thirty-seven-person Medical Response Team (and later another twenty-one-person team) to help provide emergency care for the evacuees. Never before had the federal government looked to private hospitals or health care systems to participate over an extended period in a nationally organized disaster relief effort. We took over for colleagues at the University of Texas Medical Center, who were seeing more than five hundred patients a day at a major treatment center they had set up at Houston's George Bush Convention Center. We also sent small teams of doctors and nurses to help local clinics care for survivors.[1]

During our deployment, I accompanied our team, supporting their work and making sure they were safe. Thanks to my training as a police officer, I felt I could help out in case we faced physical threats or a hostile situation. As CEO, I also would be in a position to immediately muster any resources we needed. Finally, I wanted to report on our efforts to the thirteen thousand employees back home.

It was a life-changing experience. On my second day in Houston, I arrived at the Houston Astrodome accompanied by our chief medical officer, Dr. Brent Eastman. At least a thousand cots were spread out on the floor of that giant facility—a sea of white cots occupied by survivors who had lost everything. We toured the perimeter, coming upon a large board where survivors had pinned notes in an effort to locate missing relatives. Nobody, it seemed, had been spared. We noticed cots strewn with children's toys and one where TV journalists were interviewing an elderly couple. Some people were trying to sleep—no easy task, given the terrific noise made by that many people in one space. I found myself feeling self-conscious: even though we were there to help, it felt like our team was intruding upon these people, passing through what had now become their personal space.[2]

While we were touring the Astrodome, heartbreaking stories came in from team members who were treating survivors at a nearby church. One woman with chronic breathing problems (COPD) was so sick, team member Dr. Amy Witman reported, "[she] could only speak in a whisper and only a few words at a time without gasping for air." Upon examination, her lungs seemed clear, so Witman began questioning her in search of information that might prove helpful. The woman, said Witman, "just broke down and cried. She started just sobbing and I held her. She told me stories about wading in waist-high water with dead bodies 'floating everywhere.' After a few minutes of this, her breathing improved and she was able to leave the facility."[3]

Similar scenes unfolded all around us. When authorities were transferring survivors to a new location in advance of another incoming hurricane (Rita), we spotted an elderly man in obvious distress. He had not yet packed his bags, and he was sobbing and seemed disoriented. A Red Cross volunteer tried to intercede but wasn't making much progress. Observing this scene, one of our team members was heartbroken. Another elderly woman who was treated by our team at the Bush Convention Center recounted how she had fled New Orleans before the city flooded but had been separated from her fifty-one-year-old son. Eventually he was evacuated by bus. Sadly, the bus got into an accident and flipped over, killing him. The woman was inconsolable, yet she also communicated remarkable resilience. "I usually like this time of year," she told a member of our team, "because the summer flowers start to die and I get to till the soil, knowing that fresh flowers will come back in the spring. Maybe this was my time to till the soil of my life to see what will come out one day soon."[4]

Although we had been engaged for a two-week assignment, our time in Houston was cut short by Hurricane Rita. As the city was being evacuated, some of our team managed to fly home from local airports. Given the scarcity of airline tickets, though, we were forced to fly the rest home out of Dallas. One group drove to the nearby city of College Station and arranged for small private airplanes to take them to Dallas in groups of two or three at a time. A dozen of us, myself included, had to evacuate by driving ourselves to Dallas in vans. The roads were bumper-to-bumper with people fleeing the storm, a never-ending traffic jam stretching for hundreds of miles. As the hours ticked on and Hurricane Rita neared, the situation grew tense—and frightening. We observed a burnt-out motor home, motorists stranded without gas, unscrupulous profiteers selling tap water to desperate people lacking provisions, and policemen dispatched to gas stations to keep order as supplies dwindled. After twenty-two harrowing hours, we finally arrived in Dallas. We owed a debt of gratitude to our logistics team in San Diego, who had been able to make some calls and direct us to a gas station in our vicinity that still had fuel.[5]

Sending a relief mission to Katrina marked a turning point for Scripps. As we reached out to help others in need, our employees sensed that we really were in this together, and that Scripps was something special, an employer of which we could all be proud. We discovered that a large, complex organization *can* shine when people at all levels demonstrate genuine caring. This was also the moment that our organization and its executives gained what I call "the credibility factor."

Leaders often talk about credibility and trust in terms of how transparent their communications are, how effectively they deliver results, how consistently they apply policies, and how willing they are to make courageous decisions in difficult times. Executives at Scripps value these foundations and seek to deliver on them, but we've also found that making sacrifices in times of crisis is an even more meaningful way of building deep and abiding trust with our workforce. Our organization was historically oriented toward serv-ing the wider community, but given our size, many line employees hadn't noticed. They were understandably focused on their specific tasks and facilities rather than on what the entire organization was accomplishing. Hurricane Katrina changed all that. When mem-bers of our disaster response team and I left the comfort of our offices and homes to render aid, employees saw that the organization was willing to put itself out there for a cause and that management was committed to living out its ideals. This gave the C-suite a boost of credibility that it enjoys to this day.

As a leader, you have the power to inspire your people by accepting personal risk in times of crisis and by calling upon your organization to rise up and give. That's not to say you should go around opportunistically looking for crises or take unwarranted risks for a photo opportunity. Gaining credibility was the *last thing* our executive team was concerned with when I accompanied our people to Houston. Our executive team was focused on two things:

keeping our people safe so they could serve others and document-ing what our people were doing so all of Scripps could feel like they were contributing.

Flying to ground zero of a hurricane or other natural disaster isn't for everyone. As a former cop, I have first-responder's blood, and as a leader of a health care company, I'm surrounded by doc-tors, nurses, and other caregivers with the same mentality. I bet you can find your own way of mobilizing your organization to help others in times of crisis. If you're the head of a construction com-pany, you could fly to a developing country to provide engineering support as your people help a famine-stricken village dig a new well. If you run a unit of a logistics company, you could help on scene as your team packs and ships boxes to an earthquake zone. Commit your organization to a cause and get involved in your own community proactively, so that when a situation emerges elsewhere in the world where you might help, you'll be ready to go, and you'll have built the relationships necessary to receive an assignment. The important thing in framing your personal role is to take meaningful action to protect and serve the people who work for you. They're giving back to the community, and you need to lead the way by making sacrifices of your own.

One reason leading a mission to help hurricane survivors felt so authentic for both the organization and myself was because we had spent years laying the groundwork. In the aftermath of 9/11, our leadership team at Scripps became keenly aware of how ill prepared we were to respond to a terrorist attack or natural disaster. Many hospitals were beefing up their in-hospital disaster capability, but few, if any, were building a team that could go into the community to render aid. We worried that if our region ever suffered a catastrophe, we wouldn't have resources in place to allow us to mobilize and take care of the community. To fulfill our mission, we needed equipment and specially trained employees who could assist people during the hours or days before the federal government could send disaster relief. We introduced an

Office of Disaster Preparedness and solicited volunteers for our new Medical Response Team. This office, staffed by a dedicated full-time employee, was able to secure grants that paid for some of the equipment, supplies, and training. The response team comprised physicians, nurses, and logistical and communications staff, all outfitted with vehicles, tents, satellite phones, and other equipment.

Others associated with the medical profession came to learn of our efforts, including the surgeon general, Dr. Richard Carmona. During the early to mid-2000s, Dr. Carmona and I became acquainted, and he learned about Scripps and our emergency capacities. When Hurricane Katrina devastated the Gulf States, Dr. Carmona initially informed us that any participation would need to be coordinated through FEMA, not his office. We continued to engage in discussions with the Surgeon General and the U.S. Department of Health and Human Services on how Scripps might help by contributing physicians and nurses. Eventually, we got the call that the government needed us. Our core team scrambled together and enlisted other potential caregivers. We also had to work frenetically to get travel arrangements and other logistics in place.

At the last minute, an issue arose that threatened to derail our deployment: the government wanted us to only send medical personnel, not administrative, logistics, and other support staff, including myself. I told Washington that if we couldn't send support staff as well, we couldn't deploy. It was simple: we needed to be responsible for our people. As I knew from police work, disaster areas are unpredictable. There aren't extra supplies around if you run short. Law and order can break down at any time. A team that's deploying needs to be self-sustaining. It needs protection. It needs people to help it improvise solutions on the fly. I was not about to let our people go in there unless I felt *assured* of their well-being. And I wouldn't feel assured unless we had our own people providing protection and unless I was there myself on the ground, looking out for our team and seeing to their needs.

Federal officials came around to our point of view. One of them said to a colleague, "We would never send in our people without support, would we?" A few days later, we were in Houston, deploying the team we had spent years building. It was a good thing we had administrators and logistics people along. When Hurricane Rita bore down on Houston, we found out about the mandatory evacuation at the same time as the general public, and like the general public, we were told to find our own way out. Our support staff in Houston arranged for our team's evacuation, coordinating with people back in San Diego. It was our advance planning, our on-site logistics support, and our people back in San Diego that got us out safely. Had our medical response team not had support personnel with them, the outcome could have been very different.

Make It Visible and Meaningful

When you and your organization mobilize to help the community, don't keep it a secret. Tell employees about it and offer them an opportunity to become involved. When we first learned of our invitation to deploy, we sent an email across our entire system calling for volunteers. To our delight and astonishment, more than two hundred Scripps employees wrote back over a twenty-four-hour period informing us they would like to be considered for deployment. In all, more than four hundred people applied. Obviously we couldn't take everyone, and we didn't want people to feel left out, so I decided to write daily email updates to our entire workforce letting them know what their colleagues in Houston were seeing, feeling, and doing. I also included firsthand accounts of patients the team treated. In my writing, I tried to convey some of my own emotional responses to what I was seeing. That way, I figured, if the vast majority of

Scripps employees couldn't be there with us, they could at least follow along and feel connected in spirit.

Among the stories included was one of a woman who was seen by Dr. Witman. This woman had a newborn baby boy as well as seven other children. Before evacuating, the woman had entrusted the baby to his father, who was to take him to live temporarily at his home in Georgia. The mother admitted that the baby had not been vaccinated, and she feared he might be exposed to infectious agents in Katrina's aftermath. Now that the woman was safe in Houston, she sent for the baby, but the baby's father refused to return him, and the woman to whom the father was married put the baby in foster care. The mother was "desperately trying to get him back" but unfortunately, the foster care agency was refusing to cooperate, claiming that the mother had abandoned her son. Realizing that the mother had been "acting in a selfless manner trying to protect her newborn," Dr. Witman located a social worker who might help the woman be reunited with her child.[6]

This story resonated especially strongly with our line workers. One employee wrote, "I . . . pray for the lady to regain custody of her baby. God bless all your [sic] doing for these hurting people." Another wrote that the story "brought tears to my eyes." And a third almost brought *me* to tears by writing, "What does the mother need to get her family back together? Airplane ticket, money? I can help."[7] A few days later, I was able to update our employees with happy news: the mother had in fact been reunited with her baby. A local airline had provided the mother with free air travel to Georgia while social workers apprised foster care personnel of the mother's actual circumstances. They also arranged for someone to look after the woman's other children during her trip to Georgia for family court.

It wasn't just this woman's story that connected with our employees—it was everything about our mission. One employee emailed back, "I love experiencing your Houston trip through our Scripps team's eyes. Thank you so much for keeping us a part of the team, even from home, as our 'family' works with the evacuees."[8] Others thanked me personally for taking the time as CEO to keep all the front-line staff informed; they reported that they were sharing my updates with colleagues and loved ones. Many employees were moved to put their own skills and competencies at the disposal of our team: "If there is any pharmaceutical procurement or coordination needs I can help with," one of our pharmacy buyers wrote, "please let me know!" Still other employees collected money and material goods for evacuees or wrote to say that the evacuees and our entire team were in their thoughts and prayers. One employee actually sent Scripps $10,000 to help with the relief effort. This money was used to help offset some of the hundreds of thousands of dollars we had voluntarily spent on our mission.

In the course of this undertaking, I received hundreds of responses expressing support for our efforts and deep pride in Scripps. I wish I could share all these messages with you; it's not often you see an entire community coming together before your very eyes—a nascent spirit of giving, caring, sacrifice, and true belonging. Our entire supply chain management team wished our response team safe travels and pledged, "We're here for you." An executive assistant wrote of her "tears of pride and gratefulness for the courageous and selfless efforts of all the Scripps disaster relief team." A computer programmer analyst wished "God's speed to our heroes who are also our coworkers. Be safe and take care. T-E-A-M Together Everyone Accomplishes More." One of our registered nurses asked me to thank our team and remind them that "[they] have backup at home."[9]

Reading all of these messages, I reconsidered my previous notions of what it means to build credibility as a leader. Executives in large organizations can be tempted to stage-manage their public personalities, projecting an image they think workers will respond to. You don't always have to be so deliberate or analytical; if you take the time to chronicle the good work your organization is doing *and* if you communicate in an open and emotional way, your people will respond. They won't wonder whether you're on their side; they'll *feel* viscerally that you are. Lingering resentments will diminish as your people credit the organization for the risks you've taken and the sacrifices you've made. Bring out the best in yourself, and you'll bring out the best in them too.

I should add that all of Scripps saw a boost in credibility because the media covered our efforts extensively. As members of our team arrived home after fleeing Rita, we were met by a news station wanting to interview us. Major financial benefactors who saw the coverage began calling us up to offer donations to help victims of Katrina. Nationally, we gained a reputation for being at the forefront of disaster preparedness. It was a far cry from the negative publicity we had been receiving just six or seven years earlier, when local media was writing of a "strife-ridden" health care system.[10] We had pulled together around a common cause, showing ourselves and others that Scripps, a venerable century-old institution, was back and better than ever.

Act Repeatedly

Like all efforts to engage front-line personnel, our senior leadership's involvement in our Katrina relief mission brought us closer to the Scripps workforce because it was not a one-off effort. Turning out once for a cause and then forgetting all about it communicates in a dramatic way that you're not *really* committed to your organization's highest ideals. Employees perceive that your initial efforts to sacrifice on behalf of others weren't real, just a calculated attempt to look good. They become cynical and see you as just another self-interested boss. Over time, these feelings extend to the organization as a whole. The organization's mission statement seems like empty words, and daily work loses meaning.

In our case, Katrina led naturally to subsequent relief missions in which I took on even greater personal risk. We deployed close to home in 2007 when wildfires ravaged Southern California, coordinating closely with the City of San Diego Fire Department. Around that time, we also became involved on a more permanent basis with the state of California's disaster preparedness efforts. California decided to buy three mobile hospitals for use in emergencies. Wishing to tap into what we had learned responding to Katrina, the state consulted with us to write operating protocols for the hospitals. We also helped create the structure and staffing model for the hospitals and provided both administrative and clinical teams for use in an emergency. As part of our arrangement with the state's Emergency Medical Services Authority, we agreed to be the first teams to deploy should the mobile hospital ever be needed.

A potential opportunity arose in 2010 in the wake of the earthquake that struck the desperately poor country of Haiti. We were horrified to watch the tragedy on television and see the lack of medical equipment and trained personnel on the ground. Here we were, sitting on top of a wonderful resource that could save untold lives if we could get it to Haiti. Fortunately, the California Emergency Medical Systems Authority offered the U.S. government the use of a mobile field hospital and put our clinical and administrative emergency response teams on alert.

Scripps already had experienced personnel on staff who had deployed to Katrina, but we knew we would need more help, so we put out a call for volunteers. Nearly two thousand physicians, clinicians, and support team members answered the call. We organized two teams composed of twenty nurses, twenty physicians, and fifteen support personnel and other clinicians.[11] Then we waited for the order to deploy. Unfortunately, it never came. Nine days after the earthquake, we heard definitively: the government would not be requesting the mobile field hospital and therefore would not need us to help.

We were disappointed and frustrated but soon found another potential way into action. Concerned members of the American College of Surgeons (ACS) were communicating with one another about opportunities to assist in Haiti. Surgeon Dr. Edward Gamboa, who had worked for Scripps in the past, contacted Chief Medical Officer Brent Eastman, who was on the board of regents for the ACS. Gamboa had heard about our medical response capacities at Scripps. "Look," he told Eastman, "I'm in Haiti right now. I'm very close friends with the papal nuncio [the Catholic Church's ambassador to Haiti], and if you have a team to deploy, we have a mission."

We were intrigued, but given that conditions on the ground were far more dangerous and unstable in Haiti than they had been in Katrina, we were not about to send our people in sight unseen. I decided that Eastman and I would fly to Haiti to meet with Dr. Gamboa and the papal nuncio to confirm that we had a mission suitable for our resources *and* that our team could be kept reasonably safe if deployed.

Flying on a private plane owned by John Bardis, president and CEO of the medical purchasing firm MedAssets, Eastman and I landed in Port-au-Prince about ten days after the earthquake. Even in the middle of the night, the airport was abuzz with activity as aircraft from all over the world were arriving with aid. An armored SUV owned by the papal nuncio was waiting to pick us up, complete with an armed police driver, but first we needed to check in with the Haitian authorities in the damaged airport terminal. We saw three Haitian police officers sound asleep, automatic weapons across their laps. Brent and I debated whether we should wake the men or just walk by them out of the airport. I nudged one of the police officers, and he woke with a start. He muttered some words in Creole that led us to believe he was pretty angry. When I handed him my passport, he took a quick look and casually flipped it over to one of his colleagues. "This doesn't look good," Eastman said. "Maybe we should just run."

I shook my head. "Bullets from those guns fly a lot faster than we can run." It was a tense few minutes.

Finally they stamped our passports and let us leave. We found the papal nuncio's SUV and sped through Port-au-Prince to the compound, which was located on a mountain overlooking the city. I couldn't see much of the destruction at that point, but I did see thousands of tents and makeshift shelters set up, as well as crowds of people just milling about.

We got a few hours' sleep and the next morning were driven down to the St. François de Sales Hospital, the medical facility located closest to the quake's epicenter. Nothing you might see on the news can do justice to the sight of entire neighborhoods destroyed or the stench of death lingering in the air. We encountered a seemingly endless series of tent cities; tents filled every park and open area, with thousands of people thronging the streets or lingering about. Life was beginning to get back to normal—as normal as possible in a country virtually smashed into the ground.[12] I took photographs as we drove; I was writing daily updates in a "CEO journal" for our employees back home, and these photographs would be indispensable in helping to tell our story.

A half hour later, we arrived at the hospital to find still more destruction. The main hospital building had collapsed, killing hundreds of people—including patients, staff, and visitors—many of whom were still buried in the rubble. In the central courtyard, a tent had been erected that contained whatever lab equipment workers could salvage as well as a power generator that worked intermittently. All the patients were also here; some lay on mattresses thrown on the ground, while the lucky ones occupied makeshift tents. There were no bathrooms, and only one water tap was working. A team of German and Belgian physicians as well as some nurse anesthetists and a few other first responders were caring for hundreds of people, some of whom had sustained extremely serious injuries. Hundreds of additional patients were waiting to receive care. Lacking anesthetic drugs for surgery, the medical staff was making do with only one agent, ketamine, which carried substantial risks and side effects. There was no intubation, very little use of supplemental oxygen, and exactly *one* functioning X-ray machine that stopped working whenever the power went out. Blood was scarce, and so were antibiotics, as the pharmacy that housed the supplies was just a pile of rubble. It was an especially shocking scene given that ten days had already passed since the earthquake struck.[13]

Rounding with a Belgian emergency room doctor, Brent and I came across one patient whose bicep and leg were wrapped in bandages. The Belgian doctor asked Brent, a highly respected trauma surgeon, if he knew what was wrong with the man. Brent examined him for a few moments. "Well, I think he's got compartment syndrome." Compartment syndrome can develop when a victim suffers a crush injury: the muscle can swell to the point that it cuts off blood supply, causing the extremity to die and requiring amputation. If the limb isn't amputated promptly, infections will set in and the patient will die.

"Do you know how to do the surgery?" the Belgian asked.

Brent nodded. "Yep."

The Belgian took out a red ribbon and tied it to the man's bedpost. "Good. He's your patient now. We'll show you the one operating room we have. I don't think you'll want to use it, though."

"Do I have a surgical team?"

The Belgian nodded at me. "He's your surgical team."

Brent turned to me. "Are you up for it?"

I nodded. "As long as you tell me what to do and don't let me kill anyone, absolutely."

And that's how I came to assist in my first operation. There were no other options. Unless Brent operated, the patient would lose his arm and leg or even die, and Brent couldn't operate without someone assisting him. Brent wound up performing three operations on the man, saving his life and his limbs. Over the next couple of days, we performed additional surgeries on other critically injured patients. It was an unprecedented case of a chief medical officer and a nonclinical chief executive officer collaborating directly to care for patients.

As we continued to treat patients, we were also assessing the situation, as per our plan. We made contact with leaders of

St. François de Sales and determined that Scripps could deploy a team to the hospital. With logistical arrangements with the papal nuncio in place, we decided that the security situation on the ground, although not ideal, was good enough.

The response team was quickly assembled and organized—a process made that much more efficient thanks to our experience with Katrina. Three days after our arrival, Brent and I flew home. Two nights after that, we flew back to Port-au-Prince with our response team and as many supplies as we could carry. Joined subsequently by a second team, we stayed for a week, providing care to destitute Haitians, working in conjunction with colleagues from the University of Maryland. Because we now had qualified medical personnel on site, I hung up my scrubs and ran logistics. I was proud to see our front-line doctors, nurses, and technicians in action. Our team showed true professionalism, improvising to meet any challenges that arose. Even under incredibly challenging conditions, our team was efficient, even going so far as to set up reliable medical records for patients and to organize supplies.

The sights and sounds I encountered were alternately horrific and heartwarming. One young Haitian, an engineering student, had been trapped underground and developed an ulcer that covered his entire rear end. He would have been in agonizing pain—except that he was also paralyzed from the waist down. What would happen to him? What would happen to all the men, women, and children who had lost limbs in a country where prosthetic limbs were not nearly as accessible or as advanced as they are in the United States? On the other hand, I saw needy Haitians share what little food or water they had with patients who had seen all their family members killed in the quake. Haitians suffering from broken limbs or other painful conditions sang songs rather than screaming or crying. Haitians with terrible infections or open fractures waited calmly in long lines and were grateful for the care they eventually received. Would Americans have been as respectful and patient under similar circumstances?

When helping victims of Hurricane Katrina, we hadn't been at ground zero. Sure, we had experienced the stress and emotion of dealing with survivors, but we had been in a relatively safe urban environment. This time we worked in a badly damaged building, with hundreds of dead bodies rotting nearby. We didn't have any police or soldiers protecting us. We had to look out for ourselves even as we cared for survivors. We came home recognizing how fortunate we are to live in America and to work for an organization financially and culturally strong enough to help people in need thousands of miles away. As Rob Sills, director of clinical operations at Scripps Clinic, noted, "This trip would not have been possible without all of the people back here in San Diego working every day to make Scripps as strong as it is so that we could help out no matter what the situation or the need. Everyone back home played a role in all that we did. Without my teammates stepping up and helping to carry my workload here, I would not have been able to provide care."[14]

Most of all, we were grateful for the chance to get to know the Haitian people and to support them in their time of extreme tragedy. Maureen Shackford, a registered nurse on our team, wrote that "[t]he Haitian people are some of the most stoic, graceful, beautiful, kind, and inspiring people I have ever met. . . . I am forever changed by this trip and forever grateful for being able to come along on this journey. . . . *Se gratis nou resevwa, Se tou pou nou bay*. Freely you have received, freely you give."[15] Dr. Eastman put it even more simply: "I believe I'm a better surgeon and possibly a better human being for having been [in Haiti]."[16]

Help Is on the Way

Business leaders and organizations give generously to the causes they care about, and they should be applauded for it. But in addition, we at Scripps have found that there is so much to gain when leaders become *personally* involved in providing aid in a time of crisis and when they rally their entire organization behind the effort. The most obvious and important benefit is the sense of satisfaction you get from helping someone who needs it. Beyond that, leading a relief mission is good medicine for the heart and soul of an organization. In our case, it helped an organization that had been through tough times move to new heights. It brought the mission statement and historical legacy of our organization alive as never before.

During our Katrina relief efforts, Rob Sills was walking through the Houston Convention Center when he came across a bright yellow card. A child had drawn a picture of a smiling child's face on front. Above the face were the words, "Have Hope." On the inside of the card was a picture of a heart and the words: "Help is on the way." The card touched us so much that I brought it home to share with our employees. I keep it on my desk to this day as a reminder of why we deploy in crises to help those less fortunate.

Don't just send the help. Bring it there yourself. Get out in the field to protect and serve. When it comes to getting close to your people, actions—genuine, heartfelt actions—speak louder than words.

Taking Action

To get the credibility factor working for you:

- Call upon your organization to rise up and give to others in times of crisis.
- Before a crisis emerges, commit to a cause and get involved proactively. That way you'll be prepared and ready to go when there's a call for help.
- Report back on your organization's good deeds to employees at home. Not everyone can help directly, but all employees can keep the mission in their hearts and feel proud of the organization.
- Get personally involved on the front lines in a crisis. There's no substitute for actually being there—and for genuinely caring.

Chapter Four

Tell Stories

One day in 2008, my wife, Rosemary, was walking through a Scripps facility with our family's therapy dog, Libby, when she came across a young woman being pushed in a wheelchair. The patient's eyes flicked from Rosemary to Libby, and she asked to stop and began to cry. Shocked, Rosemary asked what was wrong.

"I'm so sorry," the patient said. "It's just that . . . when I saw your dog, it hit me what happened to our family this week. Our dog just died, and I almost did too. My husband almost lost his wife, his unborn child, and his dog within weeks of each other."

As the two chatted further, Rosemary learned Miranda's story. Miranda had been pregnant with her first child and was planning on laboring at home as long as possible. At the last minute, feeling nervous, she and her husband, Bryce, decided to go to the hospital. That decision saved her life. As she was in labor, something wasn't right, so caregivers decided to deliver by emergency caesarean section. As she was wheeled toward the operating room, Miranda experienced seizures, and by the time she reached the OR, her heart had stopped. Caregivers jumped into action—over two dozen doctors, nurses, and technicians from all over the hospital. While some performed CPR, others delivered her baby. The procedure took only three minutes.

Physicians and nurses were able to get her heart beating again, but now Miranda was bleeding uncontrollably. Staff managed to stop the bleeding and put her into an induced coma. Over the next couple of days, she was given about forty different kinds of medication and twenty-five units of blood. It turned out that amniotic fluid had entered her bloodstream and Miranda had experienced a very rare allergic reaction that prevented her blood from clotting.

"I studied this condition in med school," her doctor was reported to have said, "but this was the first case I'd seen with my own eyes." In most cases, patients with Miranda's condition die. Thanks to expert care, she survived. Bryce was so grateful that he decided to give up his business painting houses and go back to school to become a nurse. He got a job as a registered nurse at Scripps and now works in the same unit where his wife's life was saved.

Incredible stories of life and death unfold every day at Scripps, but Miranda's story has taken on special meaning for our organization. A few years after her brush with death, morale in our IT department was low. The team was frustrated at having received complaints and did not feel respected. At a department meeting I attended, I realized that they didn't understand the great value they brought to the organization. "Listen," I said during the meeting, "you guys are not going to receive many notes from patients saying how much they appreciate what you do. Patients don't even think about you. They just assume that all of the technology around them will be working when they need it. But let me tell you what would happen if you weren't around."

I told them about Miranda and the life-saving treatment she had received.[1] "Let me ask you something," I said. "How did those twenty-six doctors, nurses, pharmacists, and technicians know that they needed to be in the operating room when Miranda was in crisis?"

The IT personnel looked back at me with funny looks on their faces.

"Seriously, how did they know? Was it a vibe in the air? No. It was their pagers beeping. It was the overhead call system. Who maintains those systems?"

A light bulb went off. "Well, we do," someone called out.

"Right!" I said. "What if those systems failed? Miranda needed twenty-five units of blood. Let me ask you: How did that information get communicated to the lab? It was the computer system. If the computer system had not worked, Miranda would not have received those twenty-five units." I continued in this vein, running through all the communications systems that had worked properly to support Miranda's team of caregivers. "Listen, you were in that room just as much as the doctors and nurses. You might not have been there physically, but if you had not done your jobs, Miranda would have died. You and I—because I wasn't there either—we're going to have to find satisfaction in knowing that our work *saves lives* in an indirect way. It really does." I looked around the room. "Do you get this now?"

A number of them nodded. They had gotten it. Not because I had *told* them so, but because I had dramatized the point with an emotionally engaging story.

Years later, people in that department still remind me about that story. And they still know the important role they play in patient care. They understand that they matter.

Talk About the Front Line

Storytelling is essential to the work of the front-line leader. It allows you to forge emotional connections with people, to capture their attention and communicate ideas, to invigorate and inspire them. When looking for good stories to tell, it's tempting to go outside the organization and present notable business case studies or famous anecdotes about historical figures. However, I've found that the most meaningful stories originate with the front line itself. There's no better way to help people care about an organization than by evoking the impact the organization has on real-life people. Stories about helping customers—or in our case, patients—create context for other ideas you wish to convey. They answer implicit questions about the "why" of an organization: Why are we doing this? Why does any of this matter? *Why?*

I *always* begin speeches and management meetings by talking about one of our patients and the care he or she received. I once told a group of health care executives on the East Coast what happened to Miranda. A few minutes in, I looked up and saw a nurse crying. I finished the story and continued with the more business-oriented parts of my presentation—points about health care reform, the business challenges facing heath care organizations, and so on.

After my speech, that nurse came up to say hello. "Chris," she told me, "I listen to people teaching about health care and health care administration all the time, and they never talk about the patients. And you started with a patient story that I could completely relate to. Because of that, I think I remember every point you made. You got my attention."

Because they evoke the "why" of an organization so well, stories about the care we give to patients prove especially helpful as vehicles for initiating new employees into an organization. At orientation, new employees come into the room to find pictures of people posted on all sides. We don't tell new employees at first who these people are; it might be logical to think they are members of the team these new employees are here to join. When it's my turn to speak, I'll start by saying, "See these photographs? Who are these people?" Someone in the room usually guesses they are patients. I affirm that they are and inform the new employees that these patients will be up on the wall all day long looking at them, serving as a reminder of what we are here to do.

We usually have a photograph of Claire, a vibrant young girl surrounded by volleyballs. When I ask the new employees what they think happened to her, they respond that she probably sustained a sports injury. They are shocked to hear that Claire, at the age of seventeen, was driving down the freeway when she suffered a massive stroke that completely paralyzed her left side.[2] Who ever heard of a teenager having a stroke? The ambulance took her to one of our facilities where we happened to have a brand new piece of high-tech imaging equipment and a doctor—a neuro-interventional radiologist—who hadn't yet started work at Scripps and had only happened by to obtain his physician ID badge. This doctor snaked a catheter up into her brain and was able to break up the clot that had caused the stroke. Just hours later, Claire began to recover feeling on her left side. After a period of rehab, she experienced a full recovery. Six months later she was enrolled in college, having received a volleyball scholarship.

Hearing this story, the new employees understand: Every patient has a story. These are *people*, not just patients.

During one of our quarterly system-wide management meetings, Claire and her father joined us to share their perspectives. Claire got up and told her story just as you would expect a teenager to explain it—in a simple, straightforward way, without a full awareness of her stroke's seriousness. But when it was her father's turn to speak, he broke down. The room went silent. Collecting himself, Claire's father told the group that he had been afraid he would lose his daughter or that she would become an invalid for the rest of her life. "I am so grateful," he said, "that she happened to show up in your hospital, which had the right technology and the right doctors at the right time."

I watched our managers take all this in, and I could sense from their faces what they were thinking: *We have to perform at our best so we're there for the next Claire who comes in.* Our managers, some of whom had worked in health care for decades, remembered all over again why it is they show up for work each day. Like our new employees, they apprehended through storytelling what our organization's priority is—our patients.

Now, you might argue that as a health care organization, we naturally have powerful stories to tell, whereas a B-to-B consultancy, law firm, or chain of hardware stores might not. I would counter that *every* leader has powerful front-line stories at his or her disposal, because every organization has products and services that contribute to customers' lives—otherwise the organization wouldn't exist. If you lead a team of business consultants, tell them about that time your research helped a client make a decision that allowed others to keep their jobs. If you work at a law firm, tell stories about clients' livelihoods your organization has saved. If you're a regional manager at a chain of hardware stores, talk about the elderly customers who have come in and built meaningful relationships with the clerks.

Organizations can also draw on stories of employees helping others or accounts of public service the organization renders. When one of our managers deployed to Iraq for an extended tour of duty, Scripps employees sent care packages to him and others at his camp throughout his tour. "The Scripps team sent a Santa Claus outfit at Christmas so that I was able to be Santa and deliver gifts and blank Christmas cards," our manager recalled. "A few of my marines and sailors were not getting care packages, so Scripps employees adopted them and sent gifts specifically to them.... There were packages coming every two weeks at least, and the whole camp enjoyed them. It made the time go so much quicker and brought a little bit of home to the area."[3]

As another example, in 2010 a sixty-three-year-old man collapsed during a San Diego area half-marathon. A Scripps intensive care nurse who was also running the race happened to notice the man and began CPR right away. Other physicians running nearby pitched in. Our nurse performed CPR until an ambulance drove up. The man survived. Every organization has people like this nurse; by telling their stories, you improve people's perceptions of their coworkers, affirm the values of the organization, and show your workforce that you notice and appreciate the good they are doing in the world.[4]

Tell Your Own Stories

In addition to the stories from the front lines and throughout the organization, leaders should share who they are as people. Workers in any organization want to get past a leader's title and learn about his or her values and character. They want to know: Are you like me? What do you really care about? Are you motivated by a hefty paycheck or something deeper? Why did you get into this business in the first place? Honest, heartfelt stories can evoke values and character better than mere statements ever can. They help employees see you for what you really are.

When I address our mid-level managers, I explain why Scripps matters to me by telling a haunting story from when I was a police officer. I once responded to a call at a residence to find a five-year-old boy lying on the pavement. His mother had backed out of the driveway and accidentally run over his head with her car. When I arrived she was screaming and crying, horrified at what she had done. I took one look at the boy and knew he was going to die. As he struggled to breathe, I knelt over him and cleared his airway with my fingers. A neighbor was holding the mother, telling her, "Don't worry. The policeman knows what to do. He's going to save your child's life." I continued to work on the child even though I knew my efforts were futile; I simply couldn't bear the thought of him dying in front of his mother. The boy wound up passing away the next day at a children's hospital in Los Angeles.

Today, the image of that little boy motivates me to make sure that our own people are taken care of and that we do everything possible for our patients, even if what's possible is only providing comfort. The neighbor that day was looking to me to work a miracle and save a life, and our patients look to us for the very same thing. Before it even comes to that, though, we at Scripps try to prevent bad things from happening, as policemen also do. There may be far less distance than it seems between my previous work as a cop and my current work as a health care executive. I'm on duty as CEO, and I'm responsible for what happens on my watch; it's that simple. Employees sense that my commitment to Scripps runs deep because it stems not just from my head, but also from my heart.

I have witnessed and recounted many tragedies, but effective stories don't all have to be terribly sad or serious. When I'm
addressing staff in our emergency rooms, I'll sometimes talk about
the time when I was twenty-one and working as an emergency
room clerk, and a man went ballistic. Screaming at the top of his
lungs, he jumped over the counter and threatened me and the staff
with karate moves. He was clearly out of it, possibly high on drugs.
The staff retreated, and I hit the panic button under the desk to
call for help. The guy started coming at me, and one of the doctors
shouted that he had an injection that would knock the man out.
"Chris, on three, we're just going to jump him!"

"Okay!" I shouted back.

We counted to three and jumped the guy. The doctor managed to deliver the injection. A week later, the guy came back
into the hospital and apologized, explaining that he had in fact
been on drugs.

When members of our emergency room staff hear about
this episode, they laugh and nod their heads in commiseration.
"I know what that's like," they say. "I had a situation like that
crop up just last week!" All of a sudden, I have connected with
their work in a way I never would have if I were only telling
stories relating to the C-suite. The story that opens this book,
about the hospital CEO who walked past me without saying
hello, makes a similar impact. Many of us have felt neglected or
unappreciated by our bosses; we've been at the bottom of the
pecking order and made to feel like our jobs don't matter. When
I talk about being ignored at 3:00 A.M. in a hospital basement,
workers nod their head and say, "I know how that is." Suddenly
I'm not a distant CEO to them, but an ordinary blue-collar guy
who "gets it."

Sift through your life experiences to find the most compelling
story for the group you're addressing. Look for stories with emotional content, stories that reveal something special about you,
and stories that relate well to specific work issues. Even the tiniest

anecdotes from your life can help people connect with you and feel closer to the organization you represent. Of course, don't forget to share accounts of your professional failures and good tries. One CEO I read about encourages his reports to take risks by sharing his best (or worst!) failure story and paying a bonus to managers in the room who share their stories as well.

Use Your Storytelling Skills to Explain

Storytelling can help present complex, abstract, or esoteric subjects in a way people at all levels find meaningful. As a police officer, I would routinely take troubled young people aside and paint them a vivid picture of what could happen if they didn't mend their ways. If I responded to a domestic call and encountered an otherwise good kid whom I suspected of using drugs, I would sit him down and describe to him the life he would likely have if he didn't stop partying and hanging with the wrong crowd—how he would not graduate or get a good job, would start stealing, might be forced to join a gang, and eventually would wind up either prematurely dead or in prison. I would also weave an alternate narrative of what his life *could* look like if he got serious: he might graduate, get a job, move away, see the world, and buy a house of his own. Time and again, I found that describing these mental pictures and providing broader context made an impression that helped people make better choices.

These days I take the time to create context for people around business concepts. Some new managers, for instance, don't understand what our organization's bond rating is and why it matters so much. They tune out at the very mention of it, assuming it doesn't impact their work directly. To evoke the relevance, I create a simple narrative with a series of logical steps.

"Where do we get our revenue at Scripps?" I ask. Usually someone will say "operating revenue" and I'll confirm that this is right. Another person will chime in with "philanthropy"—right again. When I ask for a third source of revenue, they'll usually remain silent. I inform them that we borrow money just like any other business would, but as a non-profit we do it by selling tax-exempt bonds.

Then I move on to the next step. When someone buys tax-exempt bonds, thus giving organizations like ours a loan, how do they know which bonds are safe and which are risky? Well, I tell our new managers, they look to the judgments put out by companies that rate bonds. The higher our bond rating, the less interest we have to pay and the less it costs us to access capital. For an organization of our size, that amounts to millions of dollars.

The question then becomes: How do we keep our bond ratings up? Well, we meet our targets and maintain consistent financial performance. So this means our bond ratings *do* matter, because the ratings reflect how successfully we're running our operations. By running their individual departments well and making their numbers, new managers can help keep our bond ratings high and our capital borrowing costs low so that we can devote more resources to our core mission. If managers miss their numbers, then our bond ratings sink and we have to divert more money to pay interest. When I take this time to unravel steps in a narrative context, new managers understand our bond ratings in a new light. It becomes relevant to them, rather than just financial jargon.

In framing narratives around business concepts, make them honest—don't invent or exaggerate stories. Also be sure to emphasize the consequences of the actions you request of your employees as well as the consequences of inaction. When I need to explain to managers and employees why their department might not get the funding they want, I begin by asking: "How do hospital administrators like me make themselves popular?"

People respond, "Well, give us more money or people."

"Right," I say. "But what happens if I spend too much money on MRI machines, CT scanners, and other fancy equipment? Our financial performance declines, which means I have to cut costs. And what's our greatest cost? People. In other words, if we buy too many toys to make people happy, in the end people *won't* be happy, because there will be layoffs. So unfortunately I can't make myself popular all the time." If I don't tell them a "story" like this that includes the ultimate consequence of a course of action, people might think I don't care about them or that I have other spending priorities. With a story like this in place, people are better able to understand the difficult decisions we make.

Explaining challenging concepts by using stories doesn't have to take place in person. We employ this tactic in many of our internal communications, most notably our newsletter *Inside Scripps*. Rather than serving only as a forum for making announcements or celebrating milestones, *Inside Scripps* also provides context about the difficult and sometimes puzzling changes taking place in our organization and industry. In recent years, we've used *Inside Scripps* to educate employees about our transformation from a hospital system to an integrated health care network. We've helped employees understand how the intricacies of health care reform affect our business. We've clarified how we allocate our resources, helping employees evaluate the financial health of our organization. We've spotlighted the parts of the business that many employees don't understand or pay much attention to, like supply chain services or laboratories. Recognizing the rising importance of visual storytelling, we also include a full-page infographic that enables readers to digest a story quickly and easily. All this being said, the best way to tell stories is still face-to-face, because that's the way the strongest personal connections are forged.

Invite Employees to Tell Stories Too

Why should leaders get to tell all the stories? They shouldn't! Scripps has built storytelling into our culture, inviting employees to craft their own narratives that imbue our organization with meaning. Our "Culture of Excellence" blog, for instance, gives employees a chance to tell stories while sharing best practices.

One employee who received medical care at Scripps wrote how she came in for an annual checkup and her doctor, calling for a mammogram, told her to contact the scheduling department for an appointment. This employee was thrilled when the scheduling department *called her* the next day to follow up, scheduling her an appointment within twenty-four hours. "Having them call me instead of me having to call to make an appointment really made me feel cared for and carried through the process."[5]

To engage employees in storytelling, try holding contests. In 2013, we unveiled a story contest called "Making It Great for Our Patients and Each Other." Winning stories were turned into videos for all of Scripps to view. Approximately fifty entries were received, including one by a supervisor at the Infusion Center at Scripps Mercy Hospital. As she related, cancer patients return to the Infusion Center multiple times to receive care, so they usually get to know staff quite well. The supervisor described one patient diagnosed with a rare, incurable cancer who was given multiple treatments over a four-year period. Sadly, we were not able to save her life. Scripps staff members were among the four hundred people who attended her memorial service. Each Scripps team member stood up to receive recognition for providing the very best care. The supervisor gave a rousing statement of our mission: "We are patient-centered and deliver quality care to every patient every time. Together We Are One!"[6] I couldn't have said it better myself.

Getting Inspired Together

I've told a handful of patient stories, but let me tell one more. At a recent management meeting we once again started the session with a patient visit and story. The medical director of our Rehabilitation Center described how this patient, a man in his thirties, had been involved in a bad motorcycle accident and was left paralyzed. He couldn't walk, and he relied on catheters for some of his critical bodily functions. When first injured, the man received good care, but his rehabilitation had left much to be desired. He came to our center and we were able to improve his condition substantially. He still couldn't walk, but he could now live a better life and even become a father.

Our rehabilitation medical director and our corporate medical director introduced this man to the audience, and he rolled out onto the stage in a wheelchair. He told the audience of six hundred people about his accident and his gratitude for the care he had received. And then the fireworks started.

"You know what?" the man said. "I'm going to walk again."

A physical therapist came on stage and strapped the man into a groundbreaking new device called an exoskeleton. This device, whose lightweight parts extend over the trunk and legs, allows a person with weakened limbs to stand and even walk.[7] With the exoskeleton helping him, picking up and putting down his legs with each step, this man slowly walked forty feet across the room. People were up out of their seats, cheering and clapping. Our CFO, a fairly serious person, leapt to his feet and shouted words of support.

When the emotion simmered down, the man explained how meaningful it was to him that he could get out of his wheelchair and walk. "I never thought this would happen again in my life." The audience applauded again as the man sat down.

That day, I was rolling out a new organizational initiative to improve the value of our care. It's a fairly abstract business topic, not necessarily the most inspiring thing to talk about, as it involves both cost reduction and quality improvement across many processes. It's also a difficult topic because I was calling on people to work harder and change familiar systems and processes.

Toward the end of the presentation, sensing that interest had waned, I tied our new initiative back to the patient we had just met. "Let me ask you something," I said to the room. "You saw this patient we had in here today. How many of you want to see more people like him walk again?"

The place erupted in applause.

"That's why we have to go forward with improving the value we deliver. If we don't change the way we work, we're never going to have the resources we need to fund the innovations that will help the next person walk. I need to know if you can go there with me. Because if you can't, I might as well give it up right now."

The applause intensified, punctuated by cheers and whoops.

Just then—I'll never forget—one of our chief nursing and operations executives jumped out of her chair. "We can do this, Chris!" she shouted. "We can do this!"

The rest of the room roared its agreement. And like that, a dull corporate initiative became exciting. As of this writing it's too early to know whether this nurse will be proven right. We're revamping processes across our organization, and we have many more still to go. But we're pulling together and making an extra effort. We're discovering the power of a good story—indeed, many of them—to transform our thinking and ourselves.

Taking Action

To tell effective stories:

- Share, through media and conversations, exceptional things employees do to serve your customers. Every organization has its heroes, and their examples can inspire us all.
- Tell inspiring stories about how the organization has given back to the community.
- Get personal. Look for honest, heartfelt stories from your own life that relate somehow to the workplace.
- Use storytelling techniques to bring complex, difficult, or esoteric subjects to life.
- Create ample opportunities for employees to craft and share their own stories.

Chapter Five

Create a Culture
of Advocacy

What makes for a great place to work? Is it just a great pay-check? Or is it an organization that has your back when a problem arises?

In 2008, trouble was brewing in the Environmental Services (EVS) department at one of our hospitals. Responding to an annual survey, employees in EVS rated the department the lowest of any in the hospital. A team met to review employee comments and figure out what was going on; that team was composed of the HR director, the department manager, and a professional from our Employee Assistance Program (EAP). EAP is a unique, in-house program in which trained psychologists help employees take action to better resolve conflicts. EAP services "range from one-on-one consultations and mediation to conflict resolution and organizational development services."[1] EAP's mission is not to take one side or the other in a dispute; rather, it's to give employees, managers, and physicians the help they need to improve their workplace. Employees often feel more comfortable and safe after working with EAP and having the delicate conversations often required to proactively solve workplace problems.

In this case, our team discovered that festering workplace conflicts were indeed behind the low scores. Staff members felt their manager was not listening to concerns they had brought forward, nor was he playing a role in resolving disputes or mediating breakdowns in communication. Nobody was backing up employees when issues arose with others outside the department, and nobody intervened when they needed new tools or equipment.

The team resolved to have the staff meet in small groups to air out their grievances and discuss what management could do to address them. Staff members proved eager to speak openly, expressing relief at finally having the opportunity to resolve long-standing issues. They created an inventory of equipment needing attention and devised a process for routinely monitoring and checking equipment for repair. Management agreed to pay more attention to the staff's input on scheduling and to consult regularly with employees in person.

Ultimately, the manager in question stepped down. In hiring a new manager, administrators made sure he was able to communicate well with the staff. Recognizing that many workers in the department have Spanish as their native language, the new manager learned Spanish and began speaking it with staff every day. He also encouraged staff members to rehearse patient interactions in English. Working together, they improved patient satisfaction and built a more hospitable work environment.[2]

This story is just one example of the hundreds of proactive interventions that EAP's six psychologists manage annually. Not all of them involve employee-management tensions. In one case, EAP intervened to help a group of five longtime female employees who had known each other for twenty years but had not been on speaking terms for the last seven. When these women were in the same room with one another, they would behave as if the others did not exist. As you might imagine, such enmity was interfering with their ability to conduct business efficiently and was poisoning the atmosphere for other workers.

An EAP counselor spent an entire day sitting down with the women individually and in groups of two or three. It turned out that a trivial slight suffered years earlier had created the conflict. At a social outing, one of the women had borrowed a small amount of money from another and had not paid it back. The woman who had given the loan didn't feel comfortable asking for the money's return. Over time, the conflict spread as the two women involved their coworkers and friends. Extensive mediation brought the five together to resolve their dispute. As the EAP counselor remembers, "I basically reminded them of what the last several years had looked like, and I asked them: How would you like the next twenty years on the job to be?" In the end, the women reconciled, walking out of the counselor's room arm in arm. They have since worked together well and have steered other employees with personnel issues to EAP for help.

I've focused on principles and tactics leaders can deploy to connect with, communicate with, and inspire line workers. We now move on to the core of the front-line leader's job: taking care of people. This responsibility applies both inside and outside the workplace, bearing on workers, their families, and the broader community. Inside the workplace, taking care of people on a fundamental level entails first and foremost *advocating for their needs*. Organizations must not merely pay a fair wage and offer significant benefits; they must also go to bat for workers, providing the resources, policies, and support that workers require to excel at their jobs. If you create a culture of advocacy in an organization—one that is evident at all times, not just when a conflict or workplace issue arises—workers feel that they're not alone. Performance improves, as does employee satisfaction and retention, resulting in happier customers and a financially healthier organization.

Manage Down

The value of a program such as EAP is substantial, but it takes much more to create a culture of advocacy. On the most fundamental level, you need a strong commitment from mid-level managers and senior leadership and, specifically, a pervasive philosophy of *managing down*. At Scripps we explicitly identify managing down as key to career success in our organization, and we include employee satisfaction ratings as an important annual evaluation metric. During our new manager orientations, I emphasize publicly that a manager's *number one job is to take care of their people.* Does everyone get the message? Sadly, no—entrenched habits die hard. One promising manager was quite capable, enthusiastic, and hardworking, but she was expending most of her energy trying to please senior management so as to position herself for promotion. Her performance metrics weren't great, and she became frustrated. We tried to let her know that cultivating relationships with her superiors would never do the trick for her; she needed to take care of her people and let the rest flow from there. But she couldn't wrap her head around it. Not long thereafter, she left the organization.

Many of our managers do get it, however, and their stories make me proud. In one case, one of our stellar occupational therapists inadvertently let her professional license expire. We expect all of our clinicians to maintain their licenses—that's their responsibility. This therapist had filled out the paperwork, written the check to pay for the required fee, put it in the envelope, stamped it, and then somehow lost the envelope under a pile on her desk. Her supervisor called the state offices and was able to arrange for the employee to overnight her payment. In addition, this supervisor met with our human resources department and made a strong case that the therapist shouldn't be disciplined; she had committed a regrettable but understandable oversight, and her performance had otherwise been exemplary. Although the employee was penalized, she appreciated how hard her manager had advocated for her.[3]

To the extent that managers *do* seem to learn how to manage down, this may be because they've seen senior leadership living this philosophy. I try to set the tone by spending part of each day responding to line employees and mid-level managers who have tried to address concerns with their bosses and failed. In one instance, an employee told me of another worker who had an idea for increasing revenues by improving our billing processes. This worker had brought the idea to her managers, but they ignored it, judging that the cost of implementing her reform would exceed the anticipated savings. I told the employee who had approached me to have her colleague send me an email explaining her idea—which she did. Her idea made sense, so I asked our financial leadership to review it. They agreed to let the employee develop a pilot program. It ultimately proved so successful that the employee transferred to a new job and is now expanding her idea system-wide.

On another occasion, I handled a concern brought up by none other than the "Thank You Man," our parking attendant who lavishes gratitude on unsuspecting patients. Because of construction at one of our hospitals, we were changing our parking configuration and had plans to install automated exit gates where the Thank You Man worked, eliminating the need for parking attendants. The Thank You Man expressed concern about his job to one of my assistants, who passed it on to me. I in turn had my assistant email another executive in charge of the parking changes. The executive told me that the Thank You Man had already been informed that his job was not being eliminated; his work assignment was just being modified. But I understood what was going on here. The Thank You Man was worried his new job wouldn't bring him into as much contact with members of the public, and he wouldn't get a chance to be the Thank You Man anymore. I handled the situation by sending a note back to the executive suggesting that we move our celebrity parking attendant to a reception area or some other place where he'd enjoy significant face time with the public.

This may seem like an excessively minor or mundane thing for a CEO to become involved with, and in a way it is. But that job shift was *incredibly* important to our parking attendant. For some reason, he wasn't getting the answers he needed to hear, and by going up the ladder, he was able to achieve resolution. This confirmed for him that Scripps was not simply another organization; it was an organization that cared. That's how a culture is built—one person and one small step at a time. In his new job, the Thank You Man will be more motivated than ever to greet everyone who passes with a smile and a thank-you, enhancing our patient experience.

Give Employees a Voice

Managing down and embedding a culture of advocacy in an organization requires an intense emphasis on *listening*. How else will you understand what your people need and want? At Scripps, we've worked hard to create numerous opportunities for people to express themselves. Many organizations (including Scripps) have open door policies, which is a good start; such policies create safe space for employees to discuss challenges. The problem, though, is that managers can take a passive role, sitting with their doors open, waiting for employees to show up. A far more effective and meaningful approach is to *proactively* solicit workers' opinions and ideas about aspects of their jobs that are and are not working.

That's exactly what Scripps managers do when they perform regular rounds with front-line workers. Rounding is as simple as stepping out of the office to talk to employees—going to them rather than making them come to you. One of our managers takes time every day to interact with her team. As she notes, these daily conversations allow her to "take the pulse" of employees; when she perceives that her people are under strain, she tries to reassure them and boost morale. Her employees have indicated how much they value her informal check-ins, noting that they now aren't afraid to approach her when troubles arise.[4] At Scripps, all managers and administrators must maintain regular rounding schedules, consulting with staff no matter what shift they happen to work.

Recognizing that rounding is not a skill that comes naturally to all managers, we provide valuable training in communication skills. Managers receive tools including note cards with phrases that might help them connect better with employees. We also train them to record conversations in a journal so that they can track the progress they're making on longer-term issues. This deliberate or structured way of handling communications helps supervisors better relate to staff, while still producing interactions that feel natural. Staff come away better able to foster welcoming and supportive employee work environments. Better communication also helps managers to meet employees' expectations (or to adjust them when necessary), enabling them to appear responsive in employees' eyes.[5] "Employees are quick to know whether you are engaged or not," manager Fritz Logan says. "They always appreciate the rounding and opportunity to communicate and share what is going on with their job, department and site."[6]

Regularly gathering groups of employees together to give feedback is another way of giving them a voice. I've mentioned already the Q&A sessions I hold. Most Fridays I also block out time in my calendar to hold casual "coffee talks" in lunchrooms or to have one-on-one discussions with employees. Likewise, for over a decade, Vic Buzachero, our corporate senior vice president for innovation, human resources, and performance management, has held focus groups with employees to learn what they think of our human resources programs. We carefully tailor our focus groups to provide a representative sample of our employees across gender, age, ethnicity, and job role. In the past, we've held groups to discuss our full range of benefits, including our health care coverage, employee recognition measures, career development options, and performance incentive programs. In 2013, about 120 employees from Scripps facilities made their voices heard in these groups.[7]

It's important to gather quantitative as well as qualitative feedback from employees. We use an employee opinion tool, our annual Great Place to Work (GPTW) survey. This survey lets employees weigh in on an array of subjects, including "workplace safety, benefits and compensation, work relationships, communication and general work environment." After more than a decade, the survey has become firmly integrated into our culture, giving rise to ongoing discussions with staff and helping leadership plan how to take action. In 2012, 94 percent of Scripps employees filled out the survey, providing data that allowed us to assess how well our organization advocates for them as compared with past years.[8]

We also email employees general questions about the organization and their work. Hundreds of employees and managers send back answers, the most memorable of which are reproduced in our monthly newsletter. In 2012, we asked employees how we might streamline our operations to better compete during an economic downturn. The responses exceeded our expectations, and included such suggestions as tightening up lab testing procedures, improving how we supply our surgical teams, and even cutting back on how much water we supply to the lawns on our grounds. We put many of these suggestions into practice, cutting expenses by thousands of dollars every year.[9]

Finally, we conduct an annual communications survey. Given how fast our organization and our industry moves, it's hard for us to know what topics our communications should cover and where we might best invest resources. Our survey gives us useful data in real time. In 2012, we learned that employees were most informed about topics like patient satisfaction, patient safety, and quality improvement, and least informed about legislative issues related to health care, information technology, and financial information. Such data allows us to better prepare our publications and online resources so that employees find them helpful and relevant.[10]

Take Employee Feedback Seriously

Don't just invite employees to tell you what's on their minds—make changes based on what you hear, so you can improve their environment. Our employee focus groups have sparked many program improvements, including "additional retirement benefits and staged retirement programs, gain-sharing for all employees, dozens of work-life balance benefits, enhanced reward and recognition programs and additional learning and career development programs designed to fill more promotions internally than externally."[11]

In 2013, employee focus groups led us to implement "Excel Together," an easy-to-use online program that allows employees to recognize other employees' great work. Using a corporate ID and password to log in, employees can salute peers in their own offices and across Scripps, using colorful eCards and eButtons to express their feelings. As of this writing, tens of thousands of eCards and eButtons have been processed through the program, with more than 75 percent of our employees receiving recognition. Not only do employees love the program, but they also feel pride in knowing that they came up with it and that responsive management put it in place.[12]

More generally, we use metrics gathered from the GPTW survey throughout the organization to gauge managers' effectiveness, which determines (along with other performance metrics) their annual bonuses. We also use these metrics to set budgets, including benefits and leadership development. For months each year after publication of the results, managers hold departmental meetings to review their scores, consulting with employees to develop action plans and identify new solutions. I personally read all two thousand pages of written GPTW comments every year, taking action with individual managers and leaders when appropriate.[13] One executive received such poor scores and comments that we had to move him into counseling. His management did not improve, and, sadly, I had to terminate him.

Far more often, other senior leaders and I report comments for use in manager evaluations and to help us track managers as they develop. During the mid-2000s, our information services (IS) department was seeing some of the lowest GPTW scores of any department, largely because any time there were issues with a technology system, staff blamed the department rather than the vendors or the system itself. In 2008, our new chief information officer, Patric Thomas, began to turn around the scores. Consulting with other senior leaders, Thomas and his management team made workforce engagement a priority, giving staff direct access to him, involving them in decision making, and improving training and equipment. He established a regular meeting called "CIO Connect" in which staff could meet with him in an informal environment. He created the CIO Advisory Team, a select group of ten staff members, to meet quarterly and provide input and guidance on departmental plans. Year after year, IS leadership collaborated with staff to establish departmental priorities. At every IS management team meeting, GPTW was a standing agenda item. All these efforts paid off. In 2013, IS had among the *highest* GPTW scores in our system. "As with many things the medium (GPTW) is the message," Thomas reflects. "Had there been no framework these efforts would not have been as focused or measurable."[14]

Over the years, comments in GPTW have also prompted our leadership team to introduce or amend a number of policies. Some of these are simple and seemingly minor: for example, in response to a comment requesting better communication, a department manager put up an information board in the middle of the unit and began sending an email update to all department members every two weeks. Others are more significant. Success Shares, our front-line incentive program for employees, was conceived by me but was advanced in part because of comments in the GPTW survey that suggested we needed to better align incentives with metrics like patient satisfaction. We also established "life cycle" benefits when we realized that staff wanted different benefits at different points in their lives and careers. We *also* created "phased retirement" as a result of GPTW comments; this allows older employees to cut back on their hours gradually, so they can maintain their medical and dental benefits while framing their work schedule as they like.

Empower Employees to Assist in Change

Advocacy entails creating spaces inside your organization for employees to improve their *own* workplaces. A good example of this at Scripps is our Workplace Empowerment ("WE") teams. In the mid-2000s, too many of our food services and maintenance people were getting injured on the job; in 2006, ninety injuries were logged at our Scripps La Jolla hospital alone, with twenty employees filing indemnity claims. We instituted a task force at this hospital to address safety issues, hoping to reduce employee injuries by 10 percent. The task force created the WE teams to figure out how people were being injured and steps we could take to prevent accidents. WE teams are run and staffed by front-line workers who understand conditions better than anyone else. We train staff members to participate, giving them the authority they need to get faulty equipment repaired and to prompt changes in work processes.[15] "We created self-sustaining safety teams that were able to report on safety issues in a non-punitive environment and gave them tools so they can quickly resolve them," reports physical therapist Lisa Golden. "The process was peer-based and informal so staff felt comfortable sharing their information regarding an injury or near miss."[16]

The WE teams proved a great success at Scripps La Jolla; by 2010, safety initiatives had decreased injuries by 40 percent among food services workers and 50 percent among environmental services personnel. Food services workers filed only two indemnity claims that year; environmental services personnel filed none. In

2011, we introduced these teams throughout our system with the goal of producing a 10 percent annual decline in indemnity claims. In 2012, we achieved this goal, saving the organization $2 million. One of our administrators observed, "This program is about saving our employees' backs—saving our employees' ability to pick up their grandchildren. And as we create a safer workplace for our employees and reduce injuries, we're also able to reduce cost for Scripps. It's the definition of a win-win."[17] Golden is equally enthusiastic. "In my now 16 years in the rehab department here at Scripps La Jolla, I have always felt my voice was heard by management. What was exciting for me during the initial pilot of the WE Team was watching other employees start to feel that same empowerment and realize the positive effect their involvement had on not only their departments but the whole hospital."[18]

We've employed similar approaches to innovate and improve a number of other areas. Our Home Health Solutions Group, created in 2008, engages our home health care service employees to identify opportunities for improvement. Group representatives hold monthly meetings to talk through suggested solutions with teams and departments. Staff in one unit noticed that many patients were having trouble navigating our automated phone answering system. Patients also let us know in their survey responses that they didn't like talking to a computer. Collaborating with the Solutions Work Group, the department discontinued the use of the automated phone system and assigned a person to answer the switchboard. It also gave company cell phones to all field clinicians so that patients could stay in direct touch about questions and concerns. Thanks to these improvements, we received fewer switchboard calls, and patients in our satisfaction surveys no longer listed "helpfulness of telephone personnel" as a major issue. "Because a person is answering our incoming phone calls, patients and staff are directed to the right person the first time," reports Susan Fischer, our director of business operations.[19]

Or consider our Scripps System Resource Services (SSRS) team, created in 2009. Demand for health care services fluctuates unpredictably over the course of the year, and as a result, we found ourselves sometimes overstaffed and sometimes understaffed. Hospitals generally deal with this problem by hiring registry or traveling nurses—and paying them at a premium—to fill temporary staffing shortages. We wanted to cut back on those costs while also providing the best possible care for patients, so we created SSRS. The team is composed of highly skilled nurses who move between Scripps hospitals in areas such as intensive care, trauma, or the operating rooms. Team members are selected on the basis of their strong identification with the Scripps mission and their interest in working in different settings with complex patients (as opposed to in a single setting, as most nurses do). When a department at one of our hospitals needs more staff for a short period, we can assign floating SSRS nurses to the job. We have since expanded the SSRS team to include pharmacists, clinicians, and even environmental services staff.

Since the inception of SSRS, we've added dozens of registered nurses to this team, slashing our expenses by $20 million annually. But the benefit goes far beyond that. Because these nurses are floating around our system, they're able to partner with our leadership teams in identifying exceptional practices and processing improvements for us to spread system-wide. One nurse was hired as a quick-response "stat" nurse and then became a supervisor in a unit that cared for patients after they had undergone surgery. Because she had worked with other such units, she was able to suggest a number of changes that dramatically improved how patients fared and how efficiently we worked, including improvement of our budgeting. SSRS "allows us to focus on patient-centric care based on quality and expertise," one of our nursing executives has noted. "Our nursing teams know our core standards and strive to improve patient and staff satisfaction."[20]

SSRS exemplifies the promise of employee-generated innovation, yet the improvements we've seen to our workplaces hardly end there. Employees throughout Scripps are constantly coming up with ways to improve what we do, and they are making change happen. Elisa Romero, a bedside registered nurse, discovered weaknesses in how colleagues were reporting on patients when they handed them off to other colleagues at the end of their shifts. With the consent of her supervisor, she investigated the process by which reports were created, consulted with other nurses on the unit, and came up with a new and better process. She and her supervisor educated staff on the new process, and leadership held staff accountable for this change. Romero's process was subsequently introduced elsewhere at her hospital and then throughout our system. She even spoke about it at a major professional conference.

"I never imagined that my recommendation could make such an impact for patient care," Romero said. "I identified an area for improvement related to patient safety and nursing communication, and leadership listened to me! I felt empowered and greatly supported. At the time I was a new nurse, and I thought that I couldn't make a difference so soon in my career, but I learned that with great guidance and support from nursing leaders and mentors, anything is possible."[21]

Give People the Tools They Need to Succeed

Employees can do so much on their own, but it's the leader's role to give them the right tools. Over the past decade at Scripps, we've introduced new resources for employees to use to handle problems, succeed in their jobs, and move ahead in their careers. Let me say a bit more about the Employee Assistance Program (EAP). Many organizations provide for the psychological health of their workforce, often by contracting with outside providers. What makes our EAP so powerful is that it's an *in-house* resource. Licensed clinical psychologists are assigned to every major facility in our network and are available to employees on a confidential basis. Because EAP staff are familiar with our HR team and managers, anyone can pick up the phone and send staff right over for immediate assistance with workplace challenges (EAP also helps employees with problems at home, as discussed in Chapter Six). This means that escalating conflicts in the workplace can be addressed in real time, before permanent damage is done. "We're able to save people from corrective action or from losing their jobs, because we're an immediate resource to help them work through their issues," EAP Director Paul Randolph says.[22]

Randolph recounts how an entire work team once showed up at his office, upset because their manager, who was new at Scripps, was driving them too hard. This manager was being tough, albeit out of a sincere desire to provide the best experience for patients. Because EAP staff was in-house, they were able to quickly bring together staff, management, and HR to talk collectively about how they might make their team work better. In this safer context, where people felt free to talk openly without repercussions, the manager was able to register the concerns of his staff and learn from them. Whereas before staff felt anxious and frustrated, now they felt like they had been heard. Everyone walked away from that experience having grown as professionals.

"Work teams are like families," EAP counselor Tarane Sondoozi notes. "We have the luxury, privilege, and honor of going into people's occupational homes, if you will, and really getting to know what makes those homes function. When you know the family and the environment and the dynamics that occur when people interact with each other, as we do, you can really help."[23]

In addition to EAP, another important resource we provide to our workforce is extensive help with career planning and development. We tell our employees that we want to become their "career destination," giving them resources so they never need to leave the organization to achieve their career goals and ambitions. We offer employees access to a wide array of academic programs, financial assistance, and career development resources. Employees can receive English-language training, education discounts, scholarships, coaching, specialty nurse programs, leadership training—to name a few. These resources are so extensive that we recently created a "Career Planning Toolkit" to help employees understand the wealth of opportunities at their disposal and how best to access them.

For quite a number of Scripps employees, the sum total of our career development programs is nothing less than life changing. "When I first joined Scripps," Senior Director of Clinical Services Michael Uzitas says, "I really was kind of one of those people that wasn't sure where I was going to go with my career . . . However in working with Scripps I was very inspired to achieve more . . . and it really made me feel like I can do this, I can make a difference."[24]

To move ahead in their careers, employees typically make use of several programs. Michelle Roberts started at Scripps as a nurse in 1998. While working full time, she went to school at night, earning both an MSN and an MBA. Scripps helped out by providing tuition assistance, scholarships, and the ability to work flexible hours. One of these programs allowed Roberts to borrow money to fund her tuition and then pay it back through subsequent work at Scripps. Today Roberts works at Scripps Green Hospital, overseeing the organ transplant program. "This organization is absolutely wonderful," says Roberts. "It allowed me to continue working, pay for most of my tuition and then pay it back by working in the position. Everyone was completely supportive and in doing all this, I actually convinced four others to go to school too!"[25]

A necessary complement to these programs—and one of our organization's strongest statements of advocacy on behalf of workers—is our public commitment to hire from within Scripps whenever possible. In 2012, 657 employees were promoted throughout the system, and more than 2,000 employees were transferred from current jobs to other positions based on where they wanted to work and what they wanted from their careers. Dual assignments allow employees to work two completely different jobs while retaining their full-time status—an option chosen by dozens of employees in 2012. We also have a program called "Other Side of the Fence" that allows employees to shadow other colleagues in different jobs in order to learn about career options at Scripps. The organization benefits from this as well, as staff members who shadow others can forge relationships that help departments work together efficiently.

Raise the Bar

At Scripps, advocacy begins with a philosophy of managing down and unfolds into policies and programs that extend throughout the entire organization. Although not all of these policies and programs will necessarily apply to your organization, as a leader you need to champion innovative measures of your own that do. If creating a far-reaching culture of advocacy seems like a tall order, keep in mind that our efforts in this area have evolved gradually and are still ongoing. We feel constant pressure to continue supporting our staff in their work, mindful that if we back down, even if only for a short while, the organization could slide backward. A culture of advocacy is like a plant—if you don't feed and water it almost every day, it will die.

All that feeding and watering really is worth it. Our numbers can confirm that an organization that has your back *is* a great place to work. In the first quarter of 2012, the average length of tenure of a Scripps employee was 9.2 years, compared with an industry average of 4.1 years.[26] In 2011, the annual employee turnover rate at Scripps was 8.6 percent, while the industry as a whole that year had a 15.9 percent turnover rate.[27] We have also received any number of awards, including inclusion on *Fortune* 100 Best Companies to Work For list every year since 2008. Our position on the list has been advancing; in 2013, we were ranked twenty-fourth in the country.

At Scripps, what we're trying to do, quite consciously, is to raise the bar for what workers can expect of management. There's no need for tension between these two parties. We in management should be taking care of workers' needs. We should be making sure that workers are treated fairly. We should be creating a culture of belonging and family. We should be giving workers a voice. We should be giving them opportunities to improve their workplace.

It's a basic fact of business: everybody at every level of an organization needs an advocate. If you're not going to step up and be that for your people, then you can't claim to be an authentic and effective leader. It's that simple.

Taking Action

To create a culture of advocacy:

- Make "managing down" your number one job, and instill that ethic throughout your organization.
- Create numerous and meaningful opportunities for employees to make themselves heard through surveys, rounding, and Q&A sessions.
- Put employee ideas into action.
- Give employees a key role in driving change.
- Create organizational practices that help employees develop their competencies and careers.
- Hire or promote from within whenever possible.

Chapter Six

Take Care of the "Me"

When I think of work experiences I *don't* want for our front-line staff, I think of my father, Harold Wilfred Van Gorder. He grew up in Hamilton, Ontario, and served in World War II as a hand-to-hand combat expert in the Canadian army. After the war, he moved to California and got a job delivering fresh milk to private homes. With the rise of supermarkets during the 1960s, not as much milk was being delivered, so his employer transferred him to a milk bottling plant. The work was physically demanding, but my father appreciated it and always did his best.

The good feelings did not last. By the 1970s, my father's body wasn't as strong or as quick as it once had been, and back injuries he received during the war were taking a toll, but he could still put in a solid day's work. Instead of making accommodations, taking into account my father's decades of dedicated service, managers at the plant made his work experience unpleasant. He never explained to my brother and me exactly what was going on, but I think he was hassled for working too slowly. I also suspect that he was forced to retire a bit earlier than he might have liked. He ended his career frustrated, perceiving that he had shown only loyalty to the company, and when he most needed loyalty back, it wasn't forthcoming.

Organizations must do better than this. We owe front-line staff care and protection, and it's in our *own* interests to provide it; as I've said all along, front-line workers are the people who are taking care of our customers. But let's get real here. Employees—and leaders, too—aren't thinking primarily about customers. They're thinking about the "me." And that's precisely as it should be. Our most important responsibilities in daily life aren't to organizations; they're to ourselves and our families. We have to provide for our kids, spouses, aging parents; work is ultimately a means to that end. If workers don't feel they have what they need to take care of their families—if they don't get paid enough or have sufficient benefits or have opportunities to advance in their careers—then they're going to leave the organization, if they can. And if they can't, they will contribute the bare minimum until they can leave.

We've succeeded at Scripps because we've done our best to take the "me" out of the equation. Pay someone appropriately, and that "me" issue vanishes. Offer programs that help employees in crisis, and that "me" is gone. Create educational programs to help employees pursue a career path—another less "me" to worry about. The fewer "me" issues you have, the more people stop feeling that they have to look out only for themselves. They come out of their cocoons and think more about others—about the organization, about customers.

Of course, one "me" issue will always loom larger than any other: "Will this organization always have a job for me? Will I be laid off?" And that's where caring for employees needs to start, with a philosophy of *avoiding layoffs except as a last resort.* Yes, you read that right. No layoffs. It's an extremely risky and controversial promise that our front-line leaders make to workers. But if they make it, they receive something extraordinary in return: strong loyalty and engagement. We at Scripps have gone for fourteen years without a single layoff, even during the Great Recession of 2008–2009. During that time we were forced to streamline operations, eliminate positions, and shift employees around, but we still didn't leave anyone jobless. The resulting goodwill is in large part responsible for the positive, high-performance culture we enjoy today. Your company can build similar goodwill if you reexamine your approach to layoffs and, more generally, take meaningful steps to demonstrate your commitment to workers' welfare.

Commit to a Philosophy, Not a Policy

I bet you're still shaking your head: *"No layoffs except as a last resort"?* For many leaders, layoffs serve as a *first* resort when companies get into financial trouble. I've taken some heat in my industry for my philosophy, with some accusing me of being foolish for taking this key cost-management lever off the table. I counter that layoffs are fundamentally unfair to workers and, frankly, just bad management.

I speak, unfortunately, from experience. In my first CEO role at Anaheim Memorial Hospital near Los Angeles, I was tasked with turning around the hospital and saving it from bankruptcy. I had spent the first part of my administrative career with that organization and knew it well, but I had left about eighteen months earlier to become COO at another hospital. During my absence, revenues had fallen and management had failed to adapt. As a result, the hospital was bleeding money and in violation of its bond insurance covenants. Our insurance company was threatening to take over the organization. When I accepted the CEO job, it was with the knowledge that I'd have to do two things: slash costs and demonstrate that we weren't going to tolerate poor performance. Because the greatest part of our costs was people, this meant for the first time in my career, I would have to orchestrate a mass layoff.

I didn't hesitate to do that. Just a few weeks after becoming CEO, I determined that we'd have to lay off several executives, roughly twenty-five managers, and dozens of the front-line staff. That cost cutting, coupled with a focus on new revenue generation, would get the hospital back to profitability within six months to a year. And so the bloodletting began. I started at the top, eliminating the chief nurse, the head of strategy, and every other senior executive except for the CFO and CEO. This was extremely painful for me, as I had worked closely with these people before and considered them my friends. Still, if I laid off front-line staff and spared leadership, I would lose credibility and kill morale, making our turnaround even more difficult.

I'll never forget calling the head of strategy, a man named Bill, into my office to deliver the bad news. Bill had worked at the hospital for more than twenty years—it was the only organization he had ever worked for—and I wasn't certain how he would react. When I told him his position had been eliminated, he rose to his feet and came around to my side of the desk. He was a big guy, and I braced for a physical confrontation. Instead, I got a bear hug. "Now I know you're going to be successful, Chris. And I know Anaheim Memorial is going to be successful." We sat down to talk about his future, and I told him that he was a smart guy who would thrive as a consultant. That's exactly what he went on to do.

Just because things worked out for Bill didn't mean I could walk away from these job cuts with my head held high. On the contrary, as the layoffs proceeded, I realized there were many people in the organization who wouldn't have the chance to bounce back as Bill had. These employees had counted on the organization to support them, and that wasn't happening. Why? Because senior leadership had failed. Changes in Medicare had reduced how much the hospital was being reimbursed, and leaders had not prepared by reducing costs and building cost-containment systems. When revenues dropped, the CEO padded the income statement by drawing on financial reserves. By the time the board knew what was happening, the organization had depleted the balance sheet and the cash on hand was below the required minimums. Workers were not to blame, but they were still losing their jobs. I thought, *I never want to have to do this again.*

Over the years, I have heard many tragic stories about the reactions employees have to layoffs. During the Great Recession, for instance, there were several incidents of murder and suicide in our local area stemming from job loss or financial stress. When I hear of violent fallout from layoffs, I've wondered how the leaders who engineered the cuts must have felt. In deciding to eliminate jobs, they probably felt convinced they were doing the right thing for the organization's long-term health, even if the cuts were painful now. What they hadn't been thinking about so much was taking care of the *people* in the organization. And as a result, everybody lost out.[1]

Such stories, my father's experience, and my tenure at Anaheim Memorial loomed large in my mind when I took over at Scripps and grappled once again with how to help an organization in crisis. Scripps was much bigger than Anaheim Memorial; I had many thousands of people for whom I was responsible. Also, I had more time at Scripps to effect change, which meant I had options at my disposal besides job cuts. I felt I needed to do better and hold myself accountable for creating a secure environment for our people. I also saw a huge hidden opportunity to remove the "me" from the equation for our people. If I was successful, I could motivate them to take the organization to places far beyond where it had been.

During my first few years, I kept the layoff card in my back pocket in case we needed it. Fortunately, we didn't. When it was clear that we had stabilized the organization, I broached the idea of adopting a permanent "no layoffs" philosophy. Our leadership team wholeheartedly supported the idea but also articulated some concerns.

"It's hard to see into the future," they told me. "If at some point down the line we have to lay people off, we would lose credibility."

I acknowledged that we would be taking a risk, but I also made sure to clarify a few things. First, I was advocating a *philosophy* of no layoffs, not a formal policy. We couldn't lock ourselves into never eliminating jobs; we had to allow for abrupt, catastrophic changes in our market—an earthquake that destroyed one of our hospitals, for instance—that might necessitate extreme measures. Second, we were not guaranteeing that workers would have exactly the same job in exactly the same location for as long as they wanted. We needed to adapt with our market, so jobs would evolve, and workers might have to accept changes if they wanted to stay employed at Scripps. Finally, I was not suggesting that a job "belonged" to a worker irrespective of performance. We would be demanding *more* performance from our managers and front-line staff and would terminate anyone who didn't rise to the occasion. But if workers did perform and were willing to adapt with the organization—if they would help us turn Scripps around—we would repay their loyalty by doing everything possible to make sure that they could stay employed with us.

We began to make job security a basic consideration when forging strategic decisions—a practice we've continued to this day. In many instances, we go to great lengths to ensure that our decisions don't rob employees of their jobs. In 2014, we had to close and demolish a chemical dependency hospital on one of our campuses to make way for a new medical office building we needed. In planning for that transition, we decided we would not lay off the thirty-five employees, many of whom had worked their entire careers at the hospital. We wound up creating a new outpatient (or "ambulatory") program, which provided jobs for the affected employees and also provided a needed service for the community. If we hadn't taken the time to plan for this change, our people would have borne the brunt of our poor decision making.

We also support our "no layoffs" philosophy by filling job vacancies with existing Scripps employees whenever possible. This has required extra effort not merely from senior executives, but also from managers throughout the organization. Don Stanziano, our corporate vice president of marketing and communications, remembers that during the recession his team held two vacancies open for managers from other departments whose positions had been eliminated. Don felt "a bit apprehensive, not sure that these individuals had the necessary skills to succeed, but also wanting to support a philosophy I believed in."[2]

Within three years, one of these employees had elected to leave Scripps, while the other had continued to grow her career on Don's team. Don reflects: "In any other organization, [the remaining employee] would have been laid off when her prior role at the hospital was eliminated. Nobody would have taken the time to recognize that she might have had skills the marketing department could use. Today she is one of our most loyal and positive staff members."[3] Don observes that preferential hiring for Scripps employees has become "part of the culture" and that most openings on his team have been filled through either vertical or lateral employee moves. All this has "created unlimited opportunities for upward mobility for staff. The word-of-mouth in our community is that Scripps is a stable place to work and any time we have an open job posted externally we are flooded with applicants telling us how badly they want to work for Scripps."[4]

Stanziano notes that the "no layoffs" approach also carries an important indirect consequence: more deliberate hiring. Since Scripps managers hire so infrequently from the outside, when they do, he says, it "forces us to be more conscious of the caliber of the talent we're hiring. It's not easy to get into Scripps because opportunities don't open up as often as they might in other organizations. When we have the opportunity to bring in new external talent, I for one have become highly selective knowing that these individuals are likely to work here for a very long time."

Stick with the Philosophy in Tough Times

"No layoffs" may be widely accepted today within Scripps, but when I first began talking about it, I'm not sure everyone understood just how serious I was. *This is just another line corporate is spinning*, some people thought. *All leaders really care about is the bottom line.* At Leadership Academy, where the conversation was more open, some of our managers expressed outright skepticism that we could really sustain "no layoffs." They had seen layoffs at other health care organizations or had read about them in the news and weren't about to fall for happy talk from the CEO. Moreover, my philosophy didn't seem to matter so much to them. Our organization was doing better and better each year. Things were looking up. Who cared about layoffs?

Then the Great Recession hit. All of a sudden, large organizations across the country were downsizing. Every day seemed to bring more bad news. Spouses and parents of employees were losing their jobs. Our own revenues weren't affected at first, but in the United States, health care usually sees a delayed impact in economic downturns, as people lose health insurance that had been attached to their jobs. As the months of recession ticked by, fears among our workforce mounted. By 2009, during my question-and-answer sessions around Scripps, employees were asking me point blank, "What's going to happen to us? Are we going to have layoffs too?"

Such questions represented a valuable opportunity for me to bring the "no layoffs" philosophy alive, remind employees of our cultural values, and define Scripps as a different kind of organization. I told our people: "Look, we're going to feel an impact from the recession. As the recession ends for everyone else, it will *start* for us. But we have a no-layoffs philosophy. That means we're going to do everything we can to keep everyone employed." In early 2009, I brought home this message by sending a memo to managers with the subject line "Assisting Our Staff." I affirmed leadership's commitment to protect jobs as much as possible, writing, "In this tough economy, we need to care about the livelihoods of our employees as we do the lives of our patients." Executive teams and department heads had to "consider layoffs only as a last resort." All managers had to show flexibility in filling "an open position with someone who has been displaced—even if you consider the applicant over-qualified or if they need additional training." I reminded managers that we needed to remain sensitive to employee anxiety and carefully manage any staffing changes; nothing less than the trust of our workforce, which we had so painstakingly built, was at stake. "Good economy or bad," I told them, "we will always succeed if we put people first—our patients and our employees."

The response I received was overwhelming. Numerous employees emailed me, thanking us for having a "no layoffs" philosophy, or expressed gratitude in Great Place to Work survey responses. One staff member wrote, "The economy as you know has taken the down right dignity of many people including a lot of Scripps employees. But even with jobs lost in the Scripps employees families and homes too, those that are fortunate enough to work for Scripps at least had a refuge a strong hold in a storm that has no end in sight."[5] Another employee told me that every single other working-age member of her family had been laid off and she was the only one who still had a job. If it weren't for Scripps, she said, they would have been out on the street.

Reading such messages, I just *knew* we were doing the right thing. I sent these notes and comments to our leadership team, so we would all continue working our hardest to protect our people.

Create Structures That Support "No Layoffs"

Although we made it through the recession without layoffs, we did have to reassign a number of employees. To accomplish this, we turned to a resource we created, the Scripps Career Resource Center (CRC). Run by human resources, the CRC is a one-stop, comprehensive support center for employees facing a job transition. Employees who enter the CRC (it is a physical location they go to during work hours) can stay for up to ninety days, receiving full pay. They are put first in line for suitable open positions and provided with necessary retraining. Full-time CRC staff members assist them with many skills relevant to their job search, such as crafting a resume, locating attractive opportunities, and handling interview questions well. Psychologists from our Employee Assistance Program provide individualized counseling to help employees deal with the emotions of a job transition.[6]

Since its founding in 2002, the CRC has assisted more than 950 employees, placing more than 90 percent in new jobs. The organization and our patients have benefited from this program, not just employees. In January 2013, Wanda Jasma, a part-time nurse and eleven-year veteran of Scripps, got the bad news that her job was being phased out. Having previously served as a manager, she entered the CRC because she wanted to remain part of Scripps. Just a few weeks later, another hospital in our system hired her as a registered nurse. Because of the CRC, we were able to retain Wanda's wealth of knowledge and experience, and we avoided the costs of severance and other benefits on top of the costs of recruiting and training a new employee.

For an organization of our size, these savings add up quickly. By keeping employees working at Scripps, we've saved over $6.8 million (and counting!) in severance payments between 2002 and 2013. This is in addition to the superior performance we get from employees like Wanda, who appreciate what the organization has done for them and are eager to give back in return.[7]

Other programs we've implemented help long-term employees nearing retirement age avoid a situation like my father's. Our staged retirement program enables employees wishing to retire gradually to cut back on their current work schedule. Eligible employees work as few as twenty-four hours per pay period, keeping their medical and dental benefits and paying the same premiums as active employees. By all accounts, participants in the program love it. Bonny Mower joined Scripps's continuing medical education department in 1982. She left seven years later but eventually returned, serving as a medical education coordinator. In her words, "Staged retirement is a great way to keep people who have experience yet let them ease into having a little more free time. I don't know of anyplace else in the world that does it. People are floored when I tell them about it."[8]

Another way we avoid layoffs and build loyalty is by encouraging staff members to constantly learn and grow as professionals. After all, an employee who has developed new skills is easier to reassign than one who has performed the same job for twenty-five years. In Chapter Five I described the wealth of resources Scripps has implemented to help employees gain new skills and advance in their careers. One program I didn't mention there (which also, incidentally, supports our efforts at standardization) is our Dedicated Education Unit (DEU). This program is designed to orient recent nursing graduates and expose them to best practices. Nurses receive forty weeks of coaching, mentoring, and training designed to transition them into clinical settings. Because of DEU, we're better able to transition nonnursing staff who have trained as nurses into new jobs. Such programs, coupled with the "no layoffs" philosophy, enable staff to think of Scripps as a true career destination. Our people feel grateful for the chance to grow and evolve with the organization over a period of years or even decades—to align their personal success with Scripps.

Care for People Beyond the Workplace

Job security and career development are some pretty big "me" issues. But people have all kinds of "me" issues that they bring with them to work. Are their parents sick? Have they lost a spouse? Are they on the verge of declaring bankruptcy? Are they in poor health? Has their home just been destroyed by a flood? Have they been a victim of a crime? Are they going through a divorce? These and any number of other issues can inhibit even the best-intentioned, most dedicated of us from performing at our best. It's in an organization's own interest to provide support and safety that extends beyond the workplace into an employee's personal life. More important, it's just the right thing to do. Once you start to see front-line staff as people, not merely as faceless employees, you want to do everything in your power to care for them. Your whole approach to leadership changes. You stop asking, "What benefits do we need to provide to remain an attractive employer?" and instead ask, "What more can we possibly do to take care of the people who do so much for us?"

The programs we offer in support of employee well-being are far more extensive than I can describe here. Our wellness benefits, for instance, are unusually comprehensive even for a health care system and include free on-site massages, free health screenings, access to an array of fitness centers, health intervention classes, cooking classes, smoking cessation programs, and much more. We sponsor a conference every year to help employees with family members facing the impending death of a loved one and another to help employees deal with parenting issues. If you're a Scripps employee, you can benefit from obtaining pet insurance at a reduced rate. If you've got young children, you get discounted childcare. After employees requested it, we introduced a benefit that reimburses parents up to $2,000 toward the costs of adopting a child.[9]

In addition to caring for our current employees, Scripps cares for our retirees in unique ways. Since January 2008, the Scripps Retiree Relations program has held an annual Service Awards event including retirees and provides access to many benefits and services, from free flu shots to educational classes to an invitation to "Scripps Night at the Ballpark." The Retiree Relations program helped prompt retired nurse Ruby Crena to come back to work. She was happy that Scripps had stayed in contact with her and that she'd received invitations to events. "It kept me thinking about coming back," she said. Although Crena enjoyed almost three years of retirement, she states "there's only so much gardening I can do." Other retirees stay active thanks to the program, volunteering in our facilities and even joining our board.[10]

Among our many programs that care for front-line staff, I'm especially proud of those that allow us to provide a safety net in times of crisis. The HOPE Fund, administered and funded by our middle managers, provides short-term, emergency cash payments to employees facing dire personal emergencies, such as serious illnesses or the destruction of their homes. The Employee Assistance Program mentioned earlier helps employees with counseling in such situations. Over time, EAP has become highly regarded at Scripps and is used to address stress management, substance abuse, legal matters, marital conflict—you name it. In 2012, EAP provided close to 3,000 sessions of help to 1,950 employees. Because EAP keeps track of the issues employees bring to the table, it is far better equipped than the usual counseling programs to intervene proactively and in a targeted way. Observing, for instance, that an increasing number of employees are suffering from depression, EAP has trained staff on how to better prevent and manage the condition.[11]

In 2009, to further coordinate crisis care for front-line staff, we created a department called Work Life Services. Despite the programs we already had in place, I felt we were falling short in supporting employees at moments of crisis (and also during moments of celebration in their lives). I would hear from local police or firefighters that a Scripps employee had been hurt, and I wished we had an internal resource that was tracking these things. I would also hear that employees going through tough times weren't even aware of all the resources we had available. I wanted us to provide support not only in cases we just happened to find out about, but in *all* cases. That meant we needed a central resource that would help employees maneuver through benefits, processes, and paperwork when a crisis occurred. I came up with the idea of creating an in-house "concierge" for employees in crisis, staffed by a dedicated, full-time employee. Yet I wasn't exactly sure what that position would encompass.

A former human resource director, Helen Neppes, stepped into the role, which we call Director of Work Life Services. Today she continues to explore and expand the role's scope. Neppes goes into action upon learning of an employee in crisis, mobilizing a multidisciplinary group of Scripps experts in benefits, case management, spiritual care, and EAP. She focuses on helping employees manage both their immediate and long-term needs and leads Scripps in doing whatever it reasonably can. "The best way to describe the development of the Work Life role," she explains, "is we keep making it up as we learn from the impact we have on employees. Each case brings something new to the table.... Helping someone fill out a form, or giving them an addressed, stamped envelope for the life insurance company is sometimes met with emotion from the person that I am helping. It's the small things."[12]

Work Life Services has proven a great relief to managers, who can return to their jobs knowing that their troubled team member is being taken care of. Employees are also happy knowing that their colleagues are in good hands. In every case Neppes has been involved with, the employee and his or her family have sent notes expressing gratitude to Neppes and Scripps for all that they did.[13]

To give you a deeper sense of Neppes's unique role and the kind of safety net we offer employees, I'll let her describe a situation that developed in 2009 before she formally stepped into her job:

> Josh Spangler's 3-month-old son Logan was in [non-Scripps] day care when he stopped breathing. Sadly, he died. Both Josh and his wife, Analee, were working at Scripps at the time. They were a young couple with a toddler daughter and had just purchased a new home, so money was tight. I was able to reach Josh's family through email and then Josh responded to me. I offered to meet him and Analee offsite

to bring him HOPE Fund documents to sign [to facilitate submission of a life insurance claim] and to discuss other relevant benefits. We decided to meet at a nearby Starbucks. When I arrived I had a card offering condolences from Chris Van Gorder and his friends at Scripps. This card had some cash in it because I felt that Josh might need it based on his current circumstances. When I approached the Starbucks I saw them sitting across from each other, sort of slumped over, and both looking down. They had coffee in front of them but they weren't drinking it or even touching their cups.

When I reached the table both Josh and his wife greeted me with hugs and then we sat down and talked about business matters—paperwork, logistics, timing. I can only imagine the pain that I saw reflected in their faces. They choked up about the card and expressed gratitude for all the support they were getting from Scripps. They appreciated me meeting them offsite. I remember thinking that if they can get through this, I certainly can. It was one of the hardest conversations that I have ever had and that includes all the cases that I have worked on since Chris's vision became a reality. . . .

Josh has since become a Director and he and Analee were blessed with another child a few years after Logan died. Josh reached out to me for support when one of his employees died a few years ago. He told me that he remembered how well we had taken care of him and his family and he wanted to make sure that his employee's family had the same experience. He was active in every aspect of crisis support and was the primary contact with the family. We had a good hug at this employee's memorial service.

When organizations step up and take responsibility for employees who are undergoing a crisis, the beneficiaries of the help naturally want to pay it forward. A virtuous dynamic of care takes hold, with employees contributing their own energies and resources to supplement the organization's. Such care becomes a recognizable part of the culture—something we all do, because that's who we are.

Give More, Get More

When I was a cop, my fellow officers and I lived by the credo that we would "leave no man behind" and "take care of our own." That freed us up to serve the community; knowing others had our backs took the most important "me" issue out of the equation. What I've learned as a CEO is that a similar credo applies just as strongly in business. The paternalistic model of the corporation providing lifetime employment and a safety net for employees is out of fashion right now, and with it, any expectation of employee loyalty. We live in a freewheeling, you're-on-your-own kind of world. But it doesn't have to be that way—and it *shouldn't* be that way. We *need* to bring back some of the old employer-employee covenant.

A job becomes more than a job when people subscribe to an organization's mission or values *and* when they feel protected and cared for. It's not transcendent, soaring rhetoric that matters but transcendent acts of kindness, big and small. No one program or benefit can ensure that people feel cared for; it's like a big jigsaw puzzle, and after a while, as more and more pieces fit into place, people say: "You know what? I see it. This really is a caring organization with a caring leadership team." And they say: "You know, if they ever call me to go to battle with them, I'm going. They were there for me, so the least I can do is be there for them." After almost fifteen years of ticking off "me" issues one by one, I feel that intense loyalty from our front-line staff. I know they have my back, too. The principle at work is simple and unmistakably human: *Give more, get more.*

I wish I could map out a logical set of steps that, if taken, would leave your organization where ours is now. Yet the safety net we've developed evolved organically and somewhat haphazardly over time. It's rooted in something I've argued for throughout this book: personal relationships with customer-facing staff. When you as a front-line leader see employees as real people and not a means to the end of higher quarterly profits, you'll feel a stronger sense of obligation to them. You'll find yourself doing things many leaders normally don't.

Sit down with your leadership team and make sure everyone embraces the notion of "no layoffs except as a last resort." Then go to your board and have the same conversation: Are we willing to stand by our commitment to employees when times get tough? If the answer is yes, start developing systems and processes and communicate what you're doing. Proceed incrementally but determinedly. You don't need a formal policy. An informal philosophy is more than enough, so long as it's coupled with meaningful actions—making it more than just words.

Just how far can you go? When we say we look out for employees, we mean until the day they die. And we look out for their family members, too. In 2012, a senior executive's mother—I'll call her Irene—learned that she had contracted an illness that would almost certainly kill her within two to five years. The executive contacted EAP to see if they could meet with his parents, who were getting a support structure in place before the disease progressed too far. That's what happened. Over the next several years, Irene, her husband, her son, and other children met regularly with Nadya, an EAP psychologist.[14] As Irene dealt with the gradual loss of her abilities and profound changes in her daily functioning and independence, her visits with Nadya became opportunities to express deep anger, pain, and grief.

Irene gradually became incapacitated, losing the ability to walk, move her limbs, or even talk. As Nadya recalls, "This person went from someone who could articulate her emotions quite well to someone who was reduced to tears and who was unable to even swallow her saliva completely." One day, when Irene was upset and physically unable to articulate what she was feeling, Nadya had an idea. "Let's switch chairs. You sit in my chair and I'll sit on the couch. Let me be you and your voice and speak for you. I'll say what I think you're feeling. If what I'm saying is accurate, then blink once. If it's not accurate, then blink twice or move your head. We'll communicate like that."

For Nadya, the role reversal was intense, beyond words. "It is one thing to sit across from someone and compassionately witness, share, and touch her pain. It's an incredible switch, a profound experience to *become* that person, to remember their story, feel it, and then reach into your heart and express what she no longer has a voice for."

As Irene became sicker, Nadya began going to her home for their sessions. With Irene's family dreading the inevitable, Nadya suggested holding an event to celebrate her life. "Why wait until she passes away for all of us to congregate and talk about how fabulous she was and be sad? Why not bring the people who love her together while she's still alive and alert so they can say whatever they want to say?"

Irene's son could not believe that Scripps EAP would foster such a compassionate and healing experience for his mother and their family. Invitations went out, and around seventy people packed Irene's house, including family members and former colleagues of Irene's from across the country. Some people were reunited with members of Irene's family after many years; others met for the first time. Food was served, and as Nadya relates, "It felt like Thanksgiving; we were all so grateful for knowing Irene and for having each other." A video was created and played that told Irene's story from birth, with photographs and commentaries from those unable to attend. Nadya passed a microphone around, asking people to share their thoughts. "Tears of joy, sorrow, and regret were shed as people told their favorite Irene stories. It felt like we were all a part of an incredible web spun around Irene."

Nadya also helped the family by creating a symbolic way for Irene to communicate with them from beyond the grave. "Irene always loved hummingbirds, so we put this story together for her to tell her young grandkids: 'Someday, I'm going to leave, and when I do, you will no longer be able to see or talk to me. But whenever you see a hummingbird, you will know that your grandma is thinking about you.'"

Irene passed away shortly thereafter. At the memorial service, Irene's son and his family thanked Scripps for helping them through these painful last years of her life. Today, Nadya looks back on this whole experience as one of the most memorable of her career. "I have used what Irene taught me to educate and train our staff and health care providers; I have facilitated and promoted other celebration-of-life events for our employees and patients. I consider it an honor and a privilege to have crossed paths with Irene and her family. Whenever I see a hummingbird, I too think of Irene."

As Nadya's statements suggests, caring for employees is deeply satisfying, above and beyond the business benefits it yields. When you give more, you do get more, first and foremost a sense of purpose and meaning. Taking care of the "me" thus becomes a virtuous cycle for organizations and individuals alike. The more you give, the more you *want* to give.

Taking Action

To take care of the "me":

- Consider embracing a philosophy of "no layoffs except as a last resort." Recommit yourself to the philosophy during tough economic times, when it really counts.
- Put resources in place to help employees retrain, gain new expertise, and grow.
- Provide for as many "me" issues as possible. Caring for employees is not limited to the workplace.
- Don't feel you need to provide a comprehensive safety net all at once. Start slowly and let the safety net develop and grow organically over time.

Chapter Seven

Hold People Accountable

When I address new managers at Scripps, one thing I explain is how our organization thinks about an employee's job. I ask managers to imagine a three-legged stool. The first leg of the stool is *responsibility*. When most people entertain taking on a new job, the first thing that comes to mind—besides the salary—are the duties they will undertake.

The second leg of the stool is *authority*. Every job comes with formal powers that we can wield in the course of executing our duties. And as we move up, we obviously get more power to go with our enhanced responsibility. I can write a $10 million Scripps check; the board has given me that authority. What would happen if our new managers tried to write a check of that size? They would probably go to jail.

The third leg . . . well, I try to build a little suspense around that one. People in an organization routinely ask for more responsibility and authority, but they never ask for more of this third element: *accountability*. Nobody has yet approached me and asked, "Would you please hold me more accountable?" And yet, the stool that represents everybody's seat at Scripps really does have three legs. If you want responsibility and authority, then you *have* to accept accountability. It's an all-or-nothing deal.

An organization can't advocate for line employees the way we at Scripps do without simultaneously requiring strict accountability for performance. Businesses have to make more money than they spend, and in competitive industries like ours we have to make sure that our people are delivering the safest, highest-quality products and services. That means holding people strictly to their numbers. Our new managers are nervous when they first hear my rule: *Miss your numbers once, you won't be around to miss them a second time.* If that sounds harsh, I would observe that a front-line executive who cares about the average worker can't afford to give a pass on poor managerial performance. If he or she does, the organization suffers and people lose their jobs. Paired with advocacy, accountability is really one of the most worker-friendly principles there is.

It comes down to this: You want the power and perks that come with a promotion? Then you'd better be prepared to deliver the results—because the organization is counting on you.

Make Leaders Formally Accountable

Like advocacy, accountability takes time to seep into an organization's culture. Don't start with entry-level workers or their supervisors—start with you, the leader, and others on your team. I discovered this during the mid-1990s, when I was a vice president watching the behavior of chief executives. From year to year we saw variations in performance. Each time the organization did not hit its targets, our CEO would make excuses. One year, when the board asked him why he hadn't met his targets, he said, "Look, this wasn't a good year. But who could have predicted what happened?" Board members accepted the excuse. They wanted to support their CEO, and the last thing they wanted to do was to expend time and effort finding a new leader.

You hear this "I couldn't have predicted" excuse often in health care, and there's a grain of truth in it: ours is a tough business, and it *is* hard to predict and manage for trends. Yet it was that CEO's *job* to be informed and attuned enough to what was happening to make smart and proactive decisions for the organization. There was no reason why he couldn't have implemented contingency plans that accounted for unfavorable scenarios. Hard as his job may have been, he was asking the board to relieve him of accountability, and that was wrong. Because he hadn't performed well, people below him in the organization were going to feel an impact and possibly get laid off through no fault of their own. Meanwhile, other workers who had also performed poorly would be disciplined by their managers, even though the same treatment was not applied to the top boss. That just wasn't fair. *All* of us should be held accountable to the same standards.

Impressed by the realization that people's livelihoods hinged on my performance, I never missed any financial or patient satisfaction targets while moving up the ranks. That changed in December 1999 when I arrived at Scripps as the chief operating officer. At the end of our fiscal year, nine months into my new job and just four months after my appointment as CEO, our organization missed its financial targets. Our financial situation was bleak. We had an operating loss of more than $20 million and only fifty-five days of cash on hand.[1]

Even though the numbers reflected my predecessor's actions rather than my own, I still took it personally and was extremely frustrated. One of the first things I did was to stop the financial bleeding by rebuilding relationships with our physicians. They were so angry at the organization's strategic direction and management's apparent tone-deafness to their needs that they had started to take their patients elsewhere. I hired a new CFO, Richard Rothberger, and together we started to make Scripps more transparent with all of our constituents, including our bankers. We had never shared our financial data openly; as a result, doctors had no clue how bad our situation was, and they didn't understand how previous funding decisions had been made. I perceived transparency as the first step toward developing more accountability for leadership and the entire organization. Rich remembers that as he sought out the financial data, he discovered that "we really didn't have very much to work with. We didn't have a bond rating so there were no external metrics that we benchmarked ourselves against. It was pretty clear that we were not in very good shape, and there had been promises to a number of people about the capital spending."[2]

We held a meeting with medical staff in which Rich delivered the grim news about our organization's finances: our operations were losing money, and we needed to embark on a turnaround. One of the doctors got up and stated that his hospital had large capital needs for imaging equipment, since some of the existing equipment was woefully out of date—how much money could Rich commit? Rich replied that there were no funds for capital improvement, and the room went quiet. Afterward, Rich was told that this was a "great presentation" because nobody in recent years had heard the truth from Scripps's finance, and Rich had delivered it point blank. The truth wasn't pretty, but at least it was the truth.[3]

To help plant the seeds of accountability for myself while reversing the fortunes of our failing organization, I worked with my team to create a plan for generating revenue during the following year. We had no need to determine a strategy running out five to ten years; we were in survival mode. Our operating plan included clear goals for which I was accountable: rebuilding relationships with our physicians, employees, and community; generating a positive operating margin; and ensuring safe and quality care for our patients. We wound up achieving all of our goals, in large part because I began holding others in the organization accountable for their performance. We adopted a second one-year plan and met those goals as well. After those first two years of hard work, our system was turning a profit.[4]

I resolved that from then on we would do everything possible to *never* miss financial targets again, and so far we haven't. Between 2000 and 2013, our annual consolidated margin increased by over 1200 percent, and that was during a historical recession that hit America's hospitals hard. In 2005 our system was granted its first bond rating of BBB+; today, we have a high AA and AA– bond rating and more than three hundred days of cash on hand.[5] We also meet broad-based goals relating to patient safety and employee relations (our "Great Place to Work" metrics). Every year, our board assesses my performance based on organizational and personal results as well as responses to a questionnaire that board members fill out. I in turn evaluate, in writing, the performance of my direct reports. Make no mistake: if I ever miss my numbers, I won't tell my board that "I couldn't have predicted" what happened. I will urge them to hold me and the team just as accountable for our performance as we do everyone else at Scripps for theirs.

Create Your Own Standards

My accountability includes my own personal set of performance metrics. I've been setting such metrics—goals that go beyond those of my organization—since I was a teenager. My family didn't have much growing up, but my parents did emphasize the importance of a strong work ethic. When I was old enough to work I felt extremely grateful to any boss who hired me. I believed that it was important to show loyalty in return and perform at my very best. Above all, I felt it was unethical for me to waste time on the job during slow periods. As my father always told me, "Never steal from the hand that feeds you." If I was being paid for a job that didn't keep me busy and I didn't find additional work to do, that was tantamount to theft.

So I made a habit of doing just a little more than everyone else did and just a little more than my employer expected. Clerking at a bookstore for minimum wage ($1.65 at the time) as a teenager, I would memorize the list of bestsellers so that when customers came in, I could appear knowledgeable and sell more books. Later, when I worked as a cashier at an Arby's, if no customers came in, the other cashiers would hang out and talk. Not me: I'd either clean tables or help out in the kitchen. I quickly moved up to shift manager—great, because I was then saving for my first car, a used 1964 Chevy Nova.

After college, when I joined the police force, sometimes my shifts were busy, with call after call coming in, but other times I found myself on patrol for hours with nobody looking over my shoulder. During the latter times, I kept busy by interfacing with the public as much as possible. When I saw teenagers loitering, I would stop and talk with them. When I saw motorists going a little too fast through a stop sign or failing to signal when turning, I would pull them over. Sometimes I'd write tickets, but my main objective was to find and arrest criminals. The greater the amount of preventative law enforcement activity I performed, the better the chances were that I would come upon people with warrants out for their arrest, people with illegal narcotics or weapons, and so on. Believing that you can't manage something you don't measure, I set myself a goal: at least one felony arrest and two misdemeanor arrests each day, supplemented by the writing of four moving violations and a couple of parking tickets.

I should emphasize that this quota was strictly personal and self-imposed. From my department's perspective, I was supposed to patrol, intervene when I saw crimes being committed, and respond to calls—that's it. It's actually illegal for police departments to set formal quotas for their officers, as you'd then risk having officers making arrests just to meet their productivity goals. I don't think I ever made any bad arrests, and I wasn't too hard on myself on days when I didn't hit my goals. The point was simply to create a mental framework that kept me working my hardest for the good of the community.

When I got into health care, I continued to do more than my job required. As department director of a hospital, I created a standard for myself of volunteering for extra assignments as they came up. In part, I was curious about different parts of the business, especially the clinical side—what the nurses and technicians did, what the protocols were, what the patients needed. But I also figured the more knowledge I had, the better I'd be able to run my own department. My drive to perform sparked criticism from other managers, who had grown lazy. But my superiors recognized me for my initiative and the skills I was developing, and they gave me even more responsibility.

Today I continue to hold myself to personal performance goals distinct from my formal, organizational metrics. A good example is response time to email. My organization doesn't have a rule that says I need to respond to every email on the same day I receive it. That's *my* standard. I don't know if I've ever failed to meet this goal; if so, it would have been on account of a technical problem. It's important to me not just because I want to respond to all emails promptly, but also because I've realized that when I fail to respond quickly, emails pile up, I get bogged down, and my performance suffers. I don't hold people around me to this same standard, because I think it's important for each of us to figure out individually what we need to do to perform at our best and commit to corresponding metrics.

Set your own performance objectives, and stick to them. Think of what your core responsibilities really are and proceed from there. Other personal goals of mine include showing up on time to every meeting. Of course, that's not always possible, but when I find myself lagging, I take responsibility in my own mind for making required changes. Think of how disruptive it would be if I regularly showed up fifteen or twenty minutes late. Not only would I waste the time of others in the meeting, but I would also inject an ethic into the culture that says being late is okay. I also set a goal of not spending much time at meetings tapping on my BlackBerry, since I know my failure to pay attention also restricts productivity (this is probably my hardest goal to meet, since it directly conflicts with my goal of rapidly responding to emails).

Establishing your own goals will push your overall performance higher and set you apart from everyone else who isn't setting goals. You'll feel satisfied to know that you really are doing the best possible job for your organization and that you're setting an example for your people to follow.

Spread the Gospel of Accountability

Once you're practicing strict accountability with yourself, the next step is to promote accountability throughout the organization and to measure it. When organizations, departments, and teams fail, many times it's because managers aren't precise in telling people what they have to do and why. You see, I don't believe the vast majority of people come to work intending to do a bad job. But when managers communicate poorly and don't follow up on key goals, employees sometimes fail to focus on objectives that really matter to an organization. Employees in these cases feel like they're working hard and that their efforts are valuable to the organization, but because they don't know or understand the organization's goals, they spend too much of their time and energy pursuing projects that have little if anything to do with these goals. Workers can lose their jobs because individuals throughout the organization are going off on their own tangents, without even realizing it.

When I first became CEO, I perceived that as a result of an almost total breakdown in communication at all levels, many mid-level managers and front-line staff didn't understand the performance metrics that counted. One nurse at Scripps Mercy Hospital, an inner-city hospital that provides a lot of charity care, told me that "not for profit" meant the hospital was supposed to lose money. I couldn't believe it; she had absolutely no understanding of the business. In truth, even not-for-profit hospitals have to generate a positive operating margin; otherwise they'll go bankrupt. When I asked her how the hospital remained open even though it lost money, she couldn't answer me. Few of her colleagues understood our system-wide goals. They were focused on their own facilities and departments, and they devoted themselves to any number of "pet" projects rather than those aligned with our system-wide goals.

To begin to change this mentality, at local and system-wide management meetings I reiterated our system-wide goals: making our budgets, delivering high-quality care (measured by patient safety, clinical outcomes, and patient satisfaction), and employee satisfaction. As the years passed, I began to tie it all together by talking about our bond ratings and why they mattered. I took that story further and explained how we sustained bond ratings—first of all, by making our budgets and hitting our strategic goals. But financial performance hinged on our having a satisfied and happy workforce—which is why making our Great Place to Work metrics mattered so much. And what about patient safety, satisfaction, and quality of care? We could have a happy workforce and hit our financial targets, but if our care quality was low and patients weren't satisfied, we were going to lose market share, and our financials would suffer (not to mention that we'd hurt patients). After learning the larger context, managers started to understand why it was so essential that they perform against these particular metrics, not just pursue whatever goals they happened to think are important.

You might ask: weren't we constraining our workforce by focusing so intensively on these key metrics? What about other things we want employees to do, like innovate? Don't we want people to work on projects they find especially enjoyable and meaningful? We do, and as I made clear to managers, they could devote their hours on the job to whatever they wanted—so long as they were first delivering on the key organizational metrics. If they wanted to spin out cool new pilot projects, great.

Delivering on core business is hard and not always the "fun" part of a job, but it is essential; otherwise the organization will get into trouble.

Lay Down the Law

Once you've created clear standards to guide organizational performance, you must enforce them. When I first started emphasizing that Scripps would be holding people accountable, managers became nervous and asked me to explain what would happen if they didn't perform well. At first I tried to answer these questions by expounding a dictionary definition of accountability. "Accountability means 'responsible or answerable to someone or for some action,'[6] so that's what we're going to do; we're going to make everyone answerable." But this was too abstract. People wanted to know: Would they be slapped on the wrist? Put on probation? Fired? So one day, I stood up in front of a group of managers and said, "You know what? Let me define accountability for you. You can miss your targets once. You won't be here to miss them twice. Simple as that. You understand what that means?" The managers looked up at me and nodded. *I get it.*

But did they? Did the message really sink in? It was one thing for me to articulate potential consequences, another thing entirely for me to set an example by actually levying them on someone. That came to pass about three years into my tenure when one of our senior leaders, Tom Gammiere, failed to make his numbers. The business unit for which he was responsible, Scripps Mercy Hospital, was not traditionally a moneymaker, but as of late it had been turning a profit and also winning awards for being a "top hospital." Tom came to me and indicated that he wanted his hospital to win a high-profile award for quality. I told him quite clearly: It would be great if his unit won that award. Fantastic. But it was a want-to-do, not a have-to-do. So he could pursue the award, but I would still hold him accountable for all organizational targets. As long as he met those numbers, he could do whatever he wanted.

Unfortunately, Tom and his team got so distracted pursuing the award that within a year Mercy went from turning a nice profit to just barely breaking even. Throughout that year, I checked in with Tom and reminded him of our organizational targets.

"No problem, Chris," he said. "We're going to hit them."

When the final numbers for the year came in, I had no choice but to call him into my office for a hard conversation.

"Tom," I said, "it looks like I have a dilemma. You and your leadership team took your eyes off of what really mattered, and as a result, I have a potential credibility problem if I don't hold you accountable. So let's see if we can find a solution."

To his credit, Tom admitted he'd failed to perform financially. "Chris, I understand the rules. We just didn't hit it this year. We'll get on it and make the numbers next year."

"Well, actually, that's not good enough," I said. "You know my philosophy. And you've now missed your targets once. I cannot let you stay here to miss them twice. It's really easy to come up with an excuse for not performing. And once I start accepting excuses for not performing, tell me the definition of a good excuse versus a bad excuse. I mean, *every* excuse becomes a good excuse. I lose credibility with the organization. Therefore, I can't accept *any* excuse for not performing."

Tom nodded gravely. But the good news was, I wasn't done.

"Look, you're a good administrator. You fell off this year, but I've got to make sure you don't miss your targets twice. You have three months to prove to me that you can get back on track. Each month for the next three months at least, I want you to come in front of the finance committee of the board and explain what it is you're doing to get the hospital back where it needs to be."

This wasn't just a slap on the wrist. By compelling Tom to come in front of the board, I was making it publicly known that he had not hit his targets. The board played its role, too, making it clear the first time Tom came before them that they were serious and expected him to return with reports of substantial progress. The next month, he did come back and report progress. The month after that, he was firmly on target, and it was clear that he was going to be able to make his numbers for the rest of the year. It was a close call, but he was able to save his job.

Looking back on that time, Tom offered several important lessons he had learned. First, it's vital to focus on items essential to the success of the overall organization. Second, staff members are frequently willing to support greater accountability. "I'll never forget announcing the hospital's turnaround plan to environmental services staff," Tom said. "After I completed covering the plan, one member of the EVS staff said to me very respectfully, 'Why didn't you come and tell us sooner? We can help you.'"[7] Finally, Tom learned the importance of the leader's role in establishing accountability. "Accountability starts at the top. It is not something that can be given away, and it must be owned by senior executives. Accountability is about recognizing what is not working and accepting the needed change, seeking help from others, and being humbled when you may be the problem.... Look in the mirror and ask, 'What do I need to do different as a leader to change the situation?' and then draw upon all the resources within and outside the organization to turn things around."[8]

From this point on, people in our organization knew that accountability mattered at Scripps and it would be enforced. "The message to me was clear," Tom says. "Scripps Mercy was going on its own path exhausting all its resources and it was out of sync with the direction the CEO and board envisioned. We needed to improve and reprioritize the organization's resources for a turnaround or they would find someone who could!"

Tom took the message to heart: ever since, he has consistently delivered solid performance. So, too, have the rest of our senior executives. Nobody has missed their major targets—not even once. And so, to the relief of our managers, I'm able to conclude my presentation on accountability by asking them: "How many people do you think I've fired based on this philosophy?" They look around in wonder, and I say, "The answer is nobody. I've never had to actually fire anybody because of this philosophy. And the reason for that is because everyone knows I would if I had to."

Provide Resources

There's a part of that last story I've left out. When I informed Tom that he had three months to put his business unit back on track, I also emphasized that I *wanted* him to succeed and that he could come see me at any time if he encountered new problems. In addition, I would deploy resources to help him out. He wouldn't be in this alone. If he was willing to put in a solid effort, the organization would be, too. As a leader, if you're going to make a point of holding people accountable, you also have to do everything you can to maximize their probability of success.

In our case, the specific resources I deployed were members of our internal consulting arm, what we call our Project Management Office (PMO). The PMO is a group of in-house consultants whose job it is to help redesign and turn around struggling parts of our business. The PMO didn't exist before I got here; we created it in 2001 because we had been spending a fortune on hiring expensive outside consultants. These consultants would come in, study a problem inside our organization, come back with a plan, and then leave it to our people to execute it. Unless we paid even more in fees, the consultants never saw the entire project through to its successful implementation. Frequently, our managers couldn't even implement it, let alone implement it well, and we got substandard results.

Moreover, we were finding that the technically or clinically brilliant people we were promoting into management roles didn't necessarily understand project management, so they would struggle to write a solid business plan and to execute on it. We needed an in-house resource that would support managers, just as our

Employee Assistance Program provided support to all managers and employees with the interpersonal parts of their jobs.

Being the ex-cop that I am, I initially called the PMO our internal "SWAT team," because we would deploy it immediately in "emergency" business situations to help managers meet their goals. The SWAT team started with one experienced hospital administrator and consultant and today has twenty-two hands on deck, most of them with graduate degrees and all of them experienced health care consultants. When managers call on PMO for help, the PMO staff member treats the engagement just as an outside consultant would, coordinating with the manager to craft an engagement plan and then working with the manager's team to produce tangible results. The manager is required to commit resources to the project so that he or she is sufficiently motivated to bring about change. PMO focuses on bringing objectivity to the problem at hand and teaching and supporting the department rather than simply doing the work for them.

We first deployed PMO in 2002 to help us turn around an affiliated organization of physicians known as Scripps Clinic. That year the Clinic was losing more than $22 million in its operations, and a swift turnaround was in order. The PMO performed a comprehensive assessment of the current state of operations and potential opportunities for improvement, reviewing data and interviewing some two dozen administrative leaders and physicians. A work plan was created, as well as clear financial targets. Work groups were convened to focus on specific areas of opportunity, and a steering committee was created that assessed and guided the work plan's execution. Corporate Senior Vice President Barbara Price recalls, "This approach focused many resources in the organization as a priority for improvement and cost reduction, in addition to focusing Clinic resources on achieving the turnaround."[9] Within twelve months, the Clinic's operations had improved and were breaking even. This is just one of many successes in which PMO has had a hand. Over the years, several key leaders have emerged from the office as well, making additional contributions to our organization.

Reward Good Performance

I've discussed what might be termed the tough-minded, *enforcement* side of accountability. But there's a softer side that's equally important: rewarding *good* performance. Many organizations do reward good performance; unfortunately, some do it in a limited way. The penalties for poor performance extend all the way down the hierarchy, while the rewards for strong performance seem to accrue primarily to those at the top. Senior leadership receives millions of dollars in bonuses or stock options for hitting short-term targets, while employees get little or nothing. In the worst cases, the policies that produced short-term gains lead to long-term problems. Guess who bears the brunt of that? Line employees—in the form of layoffs.

Look for opportunities to reward *all* your people for a job well done. It's important to maintain merit-based pay increases for front-line employees, even in tough economic times. In recent years, many in our industry have reduced pay and benefits as a way of grappling with economic uncertainty. A day might come when we can't afford to fund the kinds of merit raises we offer, but we've been able to sustain them so far—to the tune of $17 million in 2012. Even employees who have reached the top of their pay range can keep receiving increases, as we pay out their raises as lump sums. To make sure that we're properly rewarding and retaining our very best performers, we also study the labor market each spring and fall, analyzing salaries and bumping them upward if our pay scales have fallen below the competition. In 2012, 20 percent of all Scripps employees and one-third of registered nurses earned more than $90,000.[10]

In addition to salary increases, we offer performance bonuses to everyone, through a Management Incentive Compensation program as well as a popular program called "Success Shares," which rewards workers for keeping patients satisfied and our finances on track. Between 2007 and 2013, we paid out almost $50 million in Success Shares bonuses. In 2012, almost all of our employees—thirteen thousand of them—shared $10.1 million for a job well done. That year, all of our businesses delivered on their patient satisfaction numbers—a result well worth celebrating. The typical employee received almost $800, and the maximum bonus was equivalent to five days of pay. Senior leaders personally brought these checks to employees right before the holidays, which gave leadership an opportunity to warmly thank staff for their efforts.[11] In 2013, employees received as much as eight days' pay—four days for achieving productivity goals and another four days for achieving patient satisfaction goals.

I know these checks make an impression on employees, because a number of them email me each year to say thanks. "I can't even begin to tell you how grateful I am for the wonderful, wonderful gift of Success Shares," one of our executive assistants wrote. "What a blessing it is for my family, every year, no matter the amount—big or small. Over the years it has helped my family through some very tough times."[12] Another employee wrote: "So many people in power don't consider the little guy, but you always have without even a second thought!"[13] I respond to these messages by reminding our employees that although I'm glad they feel grateful, they *earned* these bonuses by performing extraordinarily well. If the organization succeeds because they've met their targets, they deserve extra compensation. It's no less a part of our philosophy of accountability than our practice of taking a hard line when employees don't perform.

Spiraling Upward

It has been years now since I began making my "three-legged stool" speech. Do all our hundreds of managers at every level meet their targets every year? No. In some cases we let managers go, and in others we reassign them, recognizing that we may bear some responsibility for putting a well-intentioned manager in a position he or she wasn't skilled enough to handle. Overall, these failures are few and far between. The message of accountability has gotten through, as evidenced by our organization's overall performance. We've achieved great things by building a culture that emphasizes excellence, cementing this culture with each round of evaluations, pay increases, and bonuses. The greatest benefactors of all this, besides our patients, have been our front-line workers, who continue to have high-quality, well-paying jobs to go to each day.

They have a supportive workplace too. I mentioned at the outset that new managers sometimes become nervous on hearing that they "won't be around to miss their targets twice." One of the best things about accountability isn't the fear it spawns, but the trust. "Look around to your left and your right," I tell our new managers. "If you can count on your colleagues to do what we ask you to do—focus and make your targets across the board—we have nothing to fear as an organization. We *cannot* fail if every manager focuses on what they have to do." That same message applies to every worker at Scripps. All of us have it in our power to pull together and produce for the good of our patients, our organization, and our careers. Almost fifteen years after our turnaround began, we haven't failed yet. We've only gotten better.

Taking Action

To hold people accountable:

- Use the "three-legged stool" concept to explain the need for accountability to your people.
- Shore up formal policies and frameworks of accountability in your organization.

- Go beyond the expectations of your job and adopt personal standards of behavior. Create metrics and hold yourself to them.
- Take action when people fail to perform. But if people genuinely want to perform and are capable of it, offer them the help they need to get back on track.
- Complement the enforcement side of accountability with meaningful rewards when people do meet their goals.

Chapter Eight

Build Loyalty and Engagement from the Middle

In August 2012, one of our environmental services workers, Elfida Vargas, took time off to attend a religious retreat in northern Mexico. Elfida and her family were supposed to travel to a rural church by van, but there weren't enough seats in the van, so they had to split up. Her daughter, son-in-law, and six grandchildren rode in the van, while Elfida and a second daughter left about twenty minutes later in a bus.

The trip began uneventfully, but soon the bus came upon a gory scene: a charred van sat by the side of the road, a number of bodies lying on the ground outside. Elfida sensed that the bodies were her family members, but prayed she was wrong. When she arrived at her destination, the pastor met her with the horrifying news: that van *was* the one her family was traveling on. It had been in a head-on collision with a truck. All eight of her family members had been killed.[1]

Back at Scripps, Elfida's manager related what had happened to his superior, who reported it to senior leadership. Just days after the accident, the organization went into action, mobilizing resources we have in place to help employees in crisis. The most important part of our response didn't come from me or other executives; it came from our middle layer of management. Elfida clearly needed counseling and time off from work, but more immediately she needed thousands of dollars to help bury and properly commemorate her eight family members. The HOPE Fund, a program conceived and administered by our middle managers, was able to provide her with the last of these. Within a week, a committee of managers had convened and wrote Elfida a check for $5,000—more than the usual amount the Fund disperses to any one person, but warranted, given the sheer magnitude of Elfida's loss.

I've described how middle managers help make values like accountability and advocacy part of daily life at Scripps. This didn't happen by chance. We created a high-performance, employee-centric culture by fostering a core group of managers who understood, embraced, and actively disseminated our strategies and organizational values and who pushed them even further by introducing structures and processes of their own. Leaders at large organizations can't touch every employee all the time. They need surrogates—people who are deeply committed to the organizational mission *and* who have daily contact with the front line. To create a worker-friendly team or organization, set an example with your own conduct at the leadership level, connect emotionally and intellectually with workers at the front line, and build loyalty and engagement from the middle.

Develop Middle Managers Yourself

I wish I could say that turning managers into cultural change agents is a simple matter of sending a memo or making an inspirational speech at your big annual meeting. It isn't. You're not just trying to set a policy here; you're trying to create a cadre of people as passionately committed to the organization as you are. Managers, by default, focus on their particular department, unit, location, team. Your task is to expand managers' perspectives by sharing with them the challenges facing the organization, your own decision-making processes, and the mission and values of the organization—so they can pass on the knowledge to the workers they supervise (as I tell our managers, their first responsibility may be to advocate for their reports, but their second is to be an effective teacher). As I've mentioned earlier, you also need to share your own leadership philosophy as well as information about the *person* behind that philosophy. You need to mentor them, modeling the kind of behavior you want them to pass on to the front line. All this means, once again, stepping outside the executive suite and taking a hands-on approach.

When I first arrived at Scripps as chief operating officer, I understood that my success rested in the hands of middle managers, but I had no experience building structures to reach across silos and mobilize managers across an entire health care system. When our embattled CEO was forced to step down six months after I arrived, I was offered his job on an interim basis. I approached members of the board and asked whether they wanted me to babysit the organization while they found a replacement or to actually run the company. Each of the board members told me, "We want you to run the company." So that's what I did. I turned to fixing a number of problems that required immediate attention, including conflict between administrators and our physicians, the financial train that was about to crash, and a leadership team that needed some work.

By June 2001, as the organization was beginning to stabilize, I turned to another problem that I had discovered as I toured locations across our network. Although decision making and accountability were excessively centralized, the cultural mindset at Scripps was decentralized and silo-oriented. Many of our hospitals had been acquired by Scripps, and we hadn't done enough to assimilate these local cultures into a bigger, Scripps culture. Also, our facilities were very different from one another. Scripps Mercy Hospital, for instance, is a central-city hospital in San Diego whose patients include very sick, low-income individuals.

Scripps Memorial Hospital La Jolla is located in the suburbs of San Diego and treats a more affluent clientele. Staff at Mercy looked at the rest of our system, including La Jolla, and thought we didn't "get" what they were doing and the challenges they faced. Staff at La Jolla looked at Mercy (which because of its low-income patient population was losing money) and thought of it as inefficient and poorly managed. Nobody saw the value of being part of a system, only the drawbacks.

What we needed to do was create an umbrella culture that would coexist with the local cultures, enriching and expanding them. If employees everywhere could take pride in being part of Scripps, then we could all be stronger and work better together. I thought about sending out a memo about the culture we wanted to build, but I didn't think that would do much. Some of our employees wouldn't even read it. Others might take it to heart but would probably forget about it in the course of their daily work.

Another possibility I already knew wouldn't work was getting in front of workers myself and making a personal appeal to them. I'd have to talk constantly to dozens or hundreds of groups in order to get the message across all our facilities. It just wasn't practical. The really influential people in our organization, I felt, were the middle management. Each manager interacted with dozens of employees, and our hundreds of managers understood on-the-ground conditions throughout the organization. If I could galvanize this group as a force for change, I'd have a powerful means of transforming Scripps into the high-performance organization I knew it could be.

At the time, we lacked any kind of structure that gave me a platform to engage regularly with mid-level managers across the organization. I turned to Elliot Kushell to help me build a program from scratch. In mid-2001 we rolled out the Scripps Leadership Academy. That might not sound especially innovative; many organizations have similarly named programs that bring in specialists to build leadership competencies. This one was much more of a personal coaching and mentorship program for managers—albeit in a group setting. And we weren't going to teach leadership in the abstract; we were going to teach leadership *at Scripps*. For so long, managers had not been well acquainted with our leadership or the decision-making process, and speculation, rumors, and distrust had taken hold. We would show managers that our corporate leaders were people too, that we cared about Scripps, and that we were making changes that would serve our organization's best long-term interests. We would invite our managers to join us in our drive to improve Scripps for patients and workers.

We started small, designing Leadership Academy as a year-long course with only twenty-five carefully selected participants at a time. Size was important, for I couldn't connect personally and build trust with a large group. Managers would meet once a month for a full day of discussions and presentations. Each session would include a two-and-a-half-hour Q&A session with me. At our first session, I would open up about myself and my career and invite managers to ask me tough questions about my leadership and what was going on at Scripps. We had only three rules: we wouldn't violate patient confidentiality, we wouldn't talk about specific personnel issues, and we wouldn't discuss an initiative if a signed confidentiality agreement was in place. Everything else was fair game.

At each subsequent session, I would return to discuss specific subjects such as accountability, staying close to front-line workers, the importance of teaching as a management activity, and policy changes in health care. This would be followed by presentations from other senior executives from across the organization (for example, finance, contracting, and the like) discussing their personal backgrounds, roles, responsibility, management style, career growth, business strategies, operational decision making, and much more. We would also have Leadership Academy participants sit in on board meetings and board committee meetings to see how decisions are made and approved for the organization as a whole. Overall, I would spend approximately one hundred hours annually interfacing with managers as part of the program.

Midway through the course, we would break managers into small teams to work on leadership projects of their choosing. We would form these teams in a deliberate way, bringing together individuals from different parts of Scripps who wouldn't ordinarily have a chance to meet and collaborate. To further build cohesion and make Leadership Academy especially memorable, we would cap off the course by holding a special graduation ceremony at which managers would present skits relating to their projects in front of hundreds of alumni, executives, and board members. We would encourage participants to make these presentations both heartfelt and entertaining, teaching them that they could make even the most serious subjects come to life. At the conclusion of the ceremony, we would hold a graduation that would include fun, surprise rituals; each year, the graduating class would wait to find out what was in store.

Leadership Academy was a rousing success that first year and has since blossomed into a signature program at Scripps, with participation considered a high honor. With each year's class, we have seen the same pattern. Most of the managers come in timid about interacting with senior leadership. They aren't sure if we really want them to challenge us with hard-hitting questions, but as the year goes on, they feel much more comfortable and end up actually competing with previous classes to ask the toughest questions. They ask about corporate finances, sensitive relations between departments—*anything*. In the process, our large and complex organization takes on a human dimension.

Surveys show that the vast majority of Leadership Academy alumni believe that participation in the Leadership Academy has aided their careers by better preparing them for leadership positions in the organization. Alumni report greater awareness of organizational goals and senior leadership's decision making; this aligns them more closely with those goals and with the Scripps mission. "When I was in Leadership Academy I would share some of the information or discussions we had around Scripps and what was happening in healthcare at my staff meetings," explained Catherine Fay, senior director of quality at Scripps Green Hospital. "After I graduated I started forwarding Chris' daily market news to the staff. Frequently, now at our staff meetings we may have discussion about something that was in the market news. I believe this has contributed to my department being well informed and engaged."[2]

Leadership Academy alumni also believe that their participation has helped them to eliminate the silo mentality and work to build a "Scripps culture" across the system. "Being a participant in the first academy class and interacting with colleagues from all over the system completely changed how I viewed my work," offered Peter Mabrey, director of medical management. "When I approached a project I began to consider how it would make an impact on the system . . . and how it would affect the culture at each hospital campus . . . By using the tools we learned from the leaders across the system who presented at leadership academy, I believe I've contributed to some of the breaking down of the silos in various areas and now see other staff also thinking 'outwardly' as well."[3]

Data suggest that Leadership Academy builds job satisfaction and Scripps loyalty: Between June 1, 2002 (a month after the first Leadership Academy class graduated) and May 31, 2007, the total turnover rate of Academy alumni was about 18 percent, with 14.5 percent turning over voluntarily and the remainder turning over involuntarily. Managers who hadn't been through Leadership Academy turned over at a rate of 34.6 percent, with 23.3 percent turning over voluntarily and 11.3 percent involuntarily.[4]

Managers who have experienced Leadership Academy remember it years later as the pivotal experience of their careers.

Some recount specific moments that won them over to cultural transformation at Scripps. For Jean Sulier, a director of rehabilitation services, it happened on the program's first day. As she tells it, she was "sitting in a room with peers from every aspect of Scripps. I looked and listened as people introduced themselves and talked about where they worked. I was truly amazed at the diversity of the people and what they did to contribute to the organization. I had no idea that many of these jobs or titles existed at Scripps, and I had been an employee for almost 13 years at the time!"[5]

Interestingly, there is one group of people inside Scripps who didn't feel comfortable with Leadership Academy at first: senior executives at our individual facilities. Some of these local leaders didn't like that I was sharing information with managers who, after all, directly reported to them, not me. Nor did they like that I was asking managers to come to me if they saw things around their facilities inconsistent with our corporate values. Admittedly, I sometimes stoked leaders' fears by joking that Leadership Academy participants knew more about current events than their bosses did. Over time, though, as our culture took shape and our organization became more successful, local Scripps leaders became more comfortable with Leadership Academy. They themselves became more aligned with senior leadership and saw the empowered, informed leaders we were creating as vital for their own success.

What's surprised me most about Leadership Academy is how much of a support it has been to me emotionally as I worked to bring change to Scripps. My job is stressful and lonely at times. When I attend a Leadership Academy meeting, I don't leave the world behind me—quite the contrary, the questions managers ask deal head-on with issues and challenges I face. But these managers respect how difficult and complex it is to run a large organization, and they appreciate my taking the time to mentor and bond with them. By the time the day is over, I invariably walk away more motivated than ever to continue working hard. *We can do this*, I think to myself. *We've got the talent to take on anything.*

Let Managers Lead

To unleash mid-level culture warriors, you have to give them real power to effect change. We've done that by creating a number of system-wide programs and events based largely on ideas put forth by Leadership Academy alumni. The first of these was a Leadership Academy alumni group. In 2002, when we graduated our first class, one of the graduates asked me, "What now?" I told him and his colleagues that they were now my "agents of culture change" and that they should demand more from the people they worked for and deliver more to the people they supervised. "Today there are twenty-five of you," I told the class, "but next year there will be fifty, and eventually, over time, the Leadership Academy alumni will be a force to be reckoned with." To that end, I suggested that the class form an alumni association to help me lead going forward.

It took a few years, but eventually the Scripps Leadership Academy Alumni Association was born. Since then, I've continued to hold monthly Q&A sessions with the group, which has become a collection of leaders that I can call on to get things done for the greater good. Members of the Association run our quarterly system-wide management meetings, organize an annual quality summit, mentor front-line employees who wish to enter the management ranks and hold important cultural events (most notably Scripps Night at the Ballpark, which attracts up to fifteen thousand people and has become San Diego's largest corporate event). "Through the Leadership Academy so many of us have been mobilized," Association member Johan Otter relates. "Otherwise, our voices would not have been heard. We are so much stronger as an organization—much better able to care for our patients."[6]

The most meaningful program that Leadership Academy alumni have put in place is the HOPE fund, the fund that helped Elfida Vargas, which originated in a project conceived of by alumni Johan Otter, Valerie Walsh, and Barbara Lorente. The three wanted to create a resource different from the benefits the organization already provided. Surveying employees, they found a strong desire for access to financial support during tough times. They looked to other organizations and found employee-run "clubs" that gathered money and time off to help employees in distress. Enlisting senior management and representatives from legal, marketing, human resources, and other departments, the three made the fund a reality. An initial effort raised $30,000 from employees in the form of small contributions. In recent years the fund has grown, collecting an additional $75,000 every year. As of 2014, the HOPE Fund has distributed more than a half million dollars in combined emergency aid and paid time off to 356 Scripps workers, including employees affected by homelessness, domestic violence, deaths of family members, and other terrible setbacks.

Elfrida Vargas is but one of many employees whose lives the HOPE Fund has touched. Another is Cynthia Sherlock, a health information technician. Diagnosed with end-stage cancer, she had been on leave for a few months and needed money from the HOPE Fund to maintain her benefits. She received the funds and eventually was able to return to work for several months, reclaiming her benefits. Sadly, her condition worsened and she prepared to leave her job for good. At a meeting with one of our managers shortly before she died, Cynthia wrote a check to Scripps for the HOPE Fund, insisting that she wanted to give something back so other employees could benefit. She expressed sincere gratitude to the HOPE Committee and the Scripps employees who contributed so she had assistance when she needed it most.

A third important program proposed by Leadership Academy participants was a similar educational group for front-line employees. Called Employee 100, this program brought front-line, hourly staff together with executives (including myself) for informational sessions about our business strategies. Just visiting a work site might allow me to meet a worker once or twice, but Employee 100 allows me to really get to know a group of employees over a period of months. Since we began this program in 2010, more than two hundred employees have graduated and become thought leaders for their teams, pushing our culture change even more effectively. One graduating class was so engaged that they gave gifts to the senior leaders who coached them and donated hundreds of dollars to the HOPE Fund.

Alumni of Employee 100 consistently describe the program as an eye-opening experience that transforms their understanding of the organization. "The real working power of the company is us," wrote pharmacy technician Jorge Murguía. "We don't realize how important our job is when we perform our tasks, it affects many levels of our company, every detail, every improvement, every task performed by us has an impact, we are a numerous group of employees and we don't think during our everyday performance that the change, the advance and the development of the hospital is in our hands."[7] Employee 100 gives our staff a sense of the broader picture. They come away not only culturally and strategically aligned, but emboldened in their jobs and eager to serve as valued teachers among their peers.

Get Personal

Although many CEOs don't have a chance to get close to middle managers and front-line staff, I count a number of them as among my closest friends and allies at Scripps and I know others on our leadership team do, too. One manager, in fact, became such close friends with us that when she experienced the tragic loss of her husband just before Valentine's Day, Rosemary and I were among the first people she called. She later spent New Year's Eve and Day at our house so as not to be alone during that holiday.

In 2005, HOPE Fund founder Johan Otter was hospitalized with severe injuries. Johan had taken time off to go on a road trip though Utah, Nevada, and Montana with his daughter. While hiking on a trail in Glacier National Park, the two were viciously attacked by a grizzly bear. They barely escaped with their lives; Johan was airlifted from the park with a fractured neck and ribs and a scalp that had been almost entirely ripped off. After being taken to a local hospital, he was airlifted again to a trauma hospital in Seattle.

When asked if he had a trauma surgeon, Johan replied that he had—our chief medical officer, Dr. Brent Eastman, whom Johan had gotten to know in Leadership Academy. "I can imagine Dr. Eastman was a bit surprised when he got a call from an emergency room in Kalispell [Montana]," Johan said.

Dr. Eastman made some calls on Johan's behalf, ensuring that he had the best care possible. Dr. Eastman, myself, and another member of our leadership team, June Komar, were so concerned about Johan that we flew up to Seattle a few days later to visit him and check on his care. "That [news that you were coming] was a single point of focus for me [as I tried] to get through that rough first week," Johan recounted. "When you came, that was enormous." We told Johan that the entire Scripps organization was behind him and that two of his managers would also come to visit the next week. He went on to make a full recovery, and as of 2014 he runs all of Scripps's employee wellness programs. "What Scripps did for me is not easily put into words," he reflects. "I have never felt more strongly cared for than during my awful bear experience."

I value Johan's gratitude, but what's truly wonderful here is that he himself has built similarly strong relationships with his own reports. Liza Blumenfeld, a veteran speech pathologist and mid-level manager, has worked for several health care systems and remarks that she has often felt "confused and abandoned" by her bosses to the point that she once considered changing professions. When she came to Scripps to work under Johan, "the mantra of unconditional support was shown early on." During her initial week in orientation, Johan took her aside and told her that "Scripps is an organization that cares for its own," handing her a card with his cell phone and home numbers and instructing her to call him anytime, day or night, with any problem big or small. The gesture meant a lot to Liza, and it set a model for her to follow as she managed her own teams.

This is by no means an isolated example. Strong working friendships have formed between many Leadership Academy alums and their reports. Wendy J. Vaughn, a patient care manager, recounts how she had been trained at another hospital to "keep her distance from the staff" and to not fraternize with them. After Leadership Academy, she began sharing her vision for her unit on a daily basis in huddles and briefings, "risking sharing with the staff what I wanted our team to dream." After her team reached an important goal, she invited her staff to a Halloween party at her house, along with their spouses and children, so they could get to know her more. "This was something I had never done before." From that point on, her team was on a roll, and morale has been high. "Whenever we see an improvement in our financial and quality metrics, we celebrate with a potluck."[8]

Share the Power—and the Credit

Just as front-line workers need the support and care of leadership, so leaders need supporters in middle management capable of and inspired to take organizational ideals and the values and bring them to life. None of us can do our jobs alone. Fortunately, our experience at Scripps shows that it's possible to build a cadre of committed managers up from scratch, *even* when you're dealing with an organization in crisis. Leadership Academy in its exact form at Scripps may not work for every organization in need of a cultural makeover, but most would benefit from a formal structure that brings leaders and managers together to share knowledge and develop mutual trust. The structure must include a safe place for regular and transparent communication; anything less won't get the job done.

At the outset of this book, I discussed how important it was to share credit for accomplishments. You now know why I'm so eager to do that when it comes to our organizational turnaround. It wasn't me who did the bulk of the work, nor was it our leadership team. It was our front-line employees and secondarily (but critically) the middle managers. Middle managers often don't get the glory in corporate America, but given what our managers have done, I'm out to change that.

There are so many managers at Scripps I could single out for glory—men and women who became strong supporters of the Scripps culture and who disseminated that culture among their teams—but I'll end this chapter by telling you about just one. When Steve Peterson joined us initially as a surgical technician, he thought of his workplace as "our little department—an island, which was sheltered from the outside world and all its activities."[9] He never thought much about that outside world; "it didn't matter much to me, because it did not affect our island . . . We just kept plugging away, alone."

Moving into a managerial role, Steve's perspective expanded beyond his department, but he still thought of his work experience as an "island," limited to the particular hospital at which he worked. He didn't see himself first and foremost as part of Scripps. Upon participating in Leadership Academy, though, his perspective fundamentally changed. "That is when the sun really came out for me. I saw the not-too-distant future. I was exposed to the strategic plan. The Scripps mission became real to me and not just a set of words on a card on my badge. I, personally, became a part of an organization and not just someone running a department in a hospital. I felt empowered to make change. I learned to be transparent to my staff. It made me a leader, rather than a manager."

Steve's experience is proof that cultivating managers as true, authentic partners can help change an organization's culture for the good. If you want to know how to become a front-line leader and drive a successful organization, don't just talk to me. Talk to Steve and the more than three hundred Leadership Academy alumni. They know too. Because they're front-line leaders themselves.

Taking Action

To build loyalty and engagement from the middle:

- Recruit managers as agents of cultural change in the organization.
- Develop formal structures that enable you to personally teach and mentor groups of managers.
- Allow managers to take a lead in proactively driving organizational change.
- Cultivate personal relationships with individual managers. Welcome them in as authentic partners.
- Give managers the recognition they deserve as the organization thrives.

Chapter Nine

Bring People Together

Have you ever gotten sick or injured and been forced to spend long hours in the emergency room? At Scripps, we knew that wait times in our ERs were growing longer; by 2007, I became frustrated that nobody in our organization seemed to be doing anything about it. Having clerked at an emergency room, I knew that we were running our ERs in the same inefficient way hospitals had thirty years earlier. At one of our facilities, 15 percent or more of patients had gotten up and left before being seen, because they couldn't stand waiting anymore.[1] Some patients with nonserious conditions were staying eight hours or longer. At times our ERs would become so full and backed up that we'd have to alert fire departments and ambulances that we couldn't take any more patients, forcing them to find alternate facilities.

In 2010, we decided we had to fundamentally redesign our ERs. The team at Scripps Mercy Hospital San Diego sat down to develop a new model of how an emergency room could operate. It wouldn't be easy to change a system that had been in place for so long, but we had to try. We wound up creating a two-track emergency room. In the old system, an access representative would first evaluate you to determine the severity and priority of your case, then a nurse would ask you what was wrong, then a another nurse, then a doctor. In the new system, we would have a doctor and a nurse triage you together just once to determine if you were among the 20 to 30 percent of ER patients who had a serious condition or the 70 to 80 percent who didn't. If you had a nonserious condition, you would then be cared for by a special team set up specifically to care for those patients, which meant you wouldn't have to wait until staff was finished caring for the more serious cases. Rather than lying on a hospital bed, which you probably didn't need and took up unnecessary space, you could wait, if you wished, in a more comfortable recliner. Only the truly sick patients would get the traditional emergency room bed, and they'd also get a team dedicated to them, able to serve them faster and better.

We rolled out the model as a pilot at Scripps Mercy and found it to be a huge success, so we spread it throughout our system. Average wait times dropped precipitously—from more than an hour and a half to less than thirty minutes. One patient at Scripps Mercy Chula Vista actually got angry because the wait time was so short; she had registered and was planning on doing her shopping while waiting to be seen. Other patients began driving long distances to our emergency rooms, knowing that they'd be seen quicker there than in their local facilities. The number of patients who left without being seen dropped to zero, and the number of times we had to turn away ambulances fell dramatically. We saw a 20 percent increase in revenue and much-improved customer satisfaction. Staff satisfaction improved, with the exception of the few nurses who just did not like this new form of patient-centered care. Those nurses left our organization.[2]

Our ER redesign was the beginning of a much larger, organization-wide effort to become both more patient-centered and more consistent in how we delivered care across our system. This effort was so successful that in just a few years it removed $200 million in costs from our system, allowing us to stay profitable and expand at a time when other hospitals were struggling and some going out of business.

How did we overcome the inertia and entrenched interests that scuttle so many change initiatives? I'll tell you what we didn't do: we didn't dictate a solution from corporate headquarters. That would only have stirred up resistance from front-line workers while also missing the chance to benefit from their valuable expertise. Instead, we mobilized the trust and openness we'd built for years, assembling a team of front-line experts including doctors, nurses, x-ray technicians, laboratory personnel—everyone who interfaced with the emergency room—as well as representatives from leadership and our project management team. Working together over a period of weeks, we expressed our different points of view, overcame areas of conflict, hammered out solutions, tested them, and celebrated our success. It was a messier process, perhaps, than traditional command-and-control, but ultimately a more effective and satisfying one. Organizations that need to change can be far more successful and innovative if they invite leaders and customer-facing personnel to make decisions together and if they put formal structures in place to sustain a productive tension between the two parties. When front-line workers are part of any solution, they own it every bit as much as leaders do. Everyone benefits—the organization, workers, and, most of all, customers.

Bridge Information Gaps

Our ability to redesign our emergency department collaboratively was especially remarkable given where we had been not so many years earlier. When I arrived at Scripps, there was so much hostility between physicians and administrators that we weren't only failing to innovate; we had our hands full just keeping the organization from imploding. The previous CEO had unveiled an ambitious plan to centralize our system and make it more sustainable, but physicians (who only worked in our facilities and were, by law, independent of Scripps) didn't like giving up control to corporate leadership; they objected to specific features of the plan and felt that the reform was being rammed down their throats.[3] Doctors at one hospital were angry because they hadn't gotten a promised infusion of capital; doctors who belonged to a large physician group didn't like how we'd handled our contracts; and doctors at a second hospital also didn't like how we handled these contracts, because the doctors in the physician group were sending patients elsewhere, thereby reducing the hospital's revenues.

The situation got so bad that medical staffs at four of our five hospitals issued formal no-confidence votes. The chairman of the medical executive committee at one hospital wrote a letter to our board expressing concern about "the deteriorating quality of patient care, ongoing loss of patient base, declining morale of bed-side caregivers and disaffection of staff physicians."[4] Initially the board stuck by the previous CEO, but when disgruntled physicians began approaching donors and telling them to withhold money, the board felt it had no choice but to ask for his resignation.

The previous CEO had created a Physicians Relations Committee to allow physicians to air their views, but it had been too late; just a few days afterward doctors began publicly calling for his removal.[5] When I took over as interim CEO, I scrapped the previous CEO's reform strategy in favor of short-term plans to improve performance and stabilize our finances. I also formed a Physicians Leadership Cabinet (PLC) cochaired by me and the chief medical officer, composed of physician leaders through-out our network, and charged with informally advising senior leadership on important operating issues. I felt hopeful that we could get physicians and administrators to work together, because I had seen it happen while serving as vice president at another hospital. Doctors there had been extremely hostile toward administrators, whom they felt had no idea what they were doing. Once some of these same doctors had been placed on the board, they came to embrace all of the decisions that they had once so vehemently opposed.[6]

That earlier experience had confirmed for me that the key to mending frayed relations was pretty simple: exposing people to better information about relevant issues. I call that "filling the gap of information." Once doctors had been privy to the same information the leadership and board received, collaboration could become a lot easier. I had seen a similar path to conflict resolution while serving as a police officer. When we were confronted with a volatile situation, such as a domestic dispute, typically the problem stemmed from a gap in how the parties understood the situation. We were trained to "bridge the gap of communication" by separating the parties, getting the full story from each, and communicating each party's story to the other. No matter how opposed people's views were, when they took the time to think about the information the other party had—information they sometimes hadn't even known about before—frequently the conflict was resolved.

In convening the PLC, I presented it explicitly to physician leaders as an opportunity for them to have open discussions and share information. I wasn't going to wield power alone; we were going to wield it together.

"You're doctors," I explained. "I'm not a physician. I need your information and opinions. Many of you weren't trained in the business of health care. That's my training and expertise. We need to share our knowledge to make better decisions. We've got to fill the gap of information, and if we do, we're going to arrive at the same decision."

Initially, physicians weren't impressed; they wanted to be designated as a board and given formal powers. I reminded them I didn't have the ability to take power from the board of trustees and give it to them. What I could do was share my own authority by consulting openly and transparently with them and asking them to share in the decision making. I pointed out that the doctors didn't have formal power to remove the previous CEO, but they had accomplished precisely that through their *informal* power—a fact that wasn't lost on me. They retorted with a challenge: "If we have all this informal power, then we want Scripps to pay us $4 million more to treat patients in the emergency room."

I knew we would have to make some financial concessions, and the doctors probably did need an increase. But $4 million was too much; our organization was losing money and had other pressing needs. Rather than say no or move straight to bargaining, I tried to bridge the gap of information around this issue.

"Listen," I said, "money is tight, and I've never learned how to spend a dollar more than once. But I also realize that without giving you an increase, we would have to close our emergency departments. So I'll give you the money you need. But if I do, I won't be able to give the nurses a raise this year. And when they ask, I'll have to say it's because I gave the resources to you."

That got the physicians' attention; they protested that this wasn't fair, but I asserted that it was. It was easy to make demands, but Scripps had limited resources and other obligations as well, so in sharing power with me they had to evaluate *all* the facts and take responsibility for the full consequences of a decision.

"Okay," they said, "let's form a task force and study this question together."

That was the breakthrough. Now the problem wasn't just mine to solve; it was theirs, too. The task force did its work, and when I convened the PLC three months later, the doctors came back with a very different attitude. Gone were the suspicion and defensiveness, replaced by a willingness to listen and help. "We think we can get along with a $2 million increase to run the emergency rooms."

Great, I thought, *we saved ourselves $2 million—money we definitely needed.*

But the doctors weren't done. "We'd like to give that other $2 million to the nurses, so they get a raise as well, and we want you to tell them that we got them that raise!"

We had a deal. This was precisely the outcome I had been hoping for: a sharing of resources between two groups that both deserved it. Most important, the doctors on the PLC owned the solution—so much so that they helped communicate our decision to the other physicians. It was a breath of fresh air for our organization—the first time in recent memory that administrators had willingly consulted with physicians on a critical issue, and the first time physician leaders felt they had a voice. Ever since, management and the board have accepted every recommendation the PLC has made, and physicians have come to the table eager to forge policy that's best for Scripps. Trust between us has deepened, and the scope of the issues we tackle has grown. As of this writing, the PLC is the most powerful body at Scripps after the board—and it doesn't even exist in our corporate bylaws.

Mobilize Collaboration Proactively

You can apply collaborative decision making to overcome conflict and pull your organization out of trouble, but the real payback comes when you mobilize it proactively to innovate and change. Leaders can develop new structures that get people working together at many levels in an organization. The potential is enormous. We've redesigned our corporate reporting structure so as to bridge what had been a yawning gap between corporate leadership and executives at our local facilities. The result—a pioneering structure called "horizontal management," which made executives responsible for functions across business units—has enabled us to stay profitable and grow in our volatile industry without so much as a single layoff.

Companies in many industries are constrained by silos that exist between key functions or disciplines. Analogously, global firms get stuck when they can't create uniform policies across far-flung business units. In medicine, excessive autonomy and fragmentation are huge problems. Doctors in the United States have generally practiced on their own or in independent medical groups; in most cases, they have not been formally employed by the hospitals or other facilities at which they worked. That might have made sense for any number of reasons, but try running a hospital when you can't make common purchasing decisions, implement uniform technologies, or promulgate standard protocols and policies. Or try running an entire health care system in which each individual hospital has the power to make its own decisions and establish practices independent of the broader system.

At Scripps, this was in part a problem of my own making. When I first became CEO, doctors had been chafing at my predecessor's attempts to take power away from the local hospitals and centralize it at corporate headquarters. Local executives were told to manage costs at their facility (hiring, purchasing, and the like) but were given no authority over many important areas of operations relating to revenue generation. As a result, apathy set in, and hospital CEOs adopted an attitude that any challenge facing Scripps was corporate's problem.

To reinstate accountability, I brought all the CEOs together and announced that I was decentralizing the organization, putting power closer to the people who actually interfaced with our patients. We'd continue to set overall strategy at corporate, but we would hand over virtually all operational decisions to leaders in the field. They would be responsible for meeting financial and patient satisfaction goals, but how they did that was up to them.

We got the accountability we wanted: our hospital CEOs all improved their operations and made their numbers. Our physicians were happier because decisions that affected them were being made on their doorstep. Yet nine or ten years into it, I realized that such decentralization was probably leading to expensive variations in how we delivered care. Some variation in how we did things made sense, but other forms didn't add value and even wasted scarce resources. Nursing practices varied so much across our campuses, for instance, that it was unsafe for us to transfer a nurse to another facility without substantial training.

MRI machines were another glaring example of how decentralization had led to inefficiency. At one of our hospitals, we had too few MRI machines, and patients were getting angry because they had to wait two weeks for a scan. The CEO of that hospital wanted to spend a couple million dollars for an MRI machine, but if you looked across our system, we had numerous MRI machines, including some that weren't being used to capacity. If we were better integrated, we could have a system in place that gave patients MRI appointments the same day, directing them to the specific facility in our system that had a machine available.

Years ago, we might have ignored such inefficiencies and simply passed it on to health insurers and patients in the form of higher prices. But passage of the Affordable Care Act started putting new pressure on hospitals to make health care more affordable while sustaining or even improving quality. Looking ahead, I knew that the reimbursements we'd receive from government and private insurers to cover the care we provide would flatten or even decrease. If we were going to remain viable as a system, we had to somehow cut costs. I was determined to avoid layoffs, so I would have to cut costs by standardizing more of what we did so as to realize efficiencies. The complication was how to standardize our operations without losing the sense of accountability we'd instilled at the local level. Was it possible to be both integrated and localized at the same time?

I puzzled over this dilemma for quite some time. The answer came to me in 2010, when we were deployed to Haiti to help victims of the earthquake. One morning I was standing at the papal nuncio's compound on Mount Calvary overlooking the city of Port-au-Prince. It was a bright day, with blue sky and sea stretching to the horizon and white buildings glimmering below. *How beautiful*, I thought, and then immediately chastised myself. The previous day we had driven into the city and seen the destroyed buildings and the desperate people. How could this be beautiful?

That contradiction represented the germ of an idea. From this height, you couldn't see any of the devastation. But that was true for Scripps as well: when I or the CEOs at our hospitals looked down on our organizations, everything looked wonderful—things seemed to be working, we were hitting our bottom lines, and our employees and physicians were happy. But if you looked *horizontally* across our system, you saw a very different picture: significant waste owing to excessive lack of coordination in practices. The vertical perspective remained important, as we needed to make decisions that reflected on-the-ground realities at our diverse facilities. What we needed to do was systematically *marry* the horizontal and the vertical, approaching decisions and reevaluating our operations with both perspectives in mind. Just as we had used the PLC to create dialogue between physicians and leadership, we had to create a reporting structure that narrowed the gap of information between executives managing from on high and other executives who oversaw just a segment of operations (nursing, home health, facilities design and construction, and so on).

Intrigued by the horizontal perspective, I asked our project management team to look across our system, analyze variations in practice, and figure out how much money we were wasting. The answer came back: a staggering $150 million. I knew we probably couldn't save all of that, but even a portion was an alluring enough prize to warrant a new organizational structure. I wound up creating a "matrix" organization that teamed traditional "vertically minded" executives with those who would be responsible for a slice of operations. CEOs and campus managers at our local facilities would play the vertical roles; because they were on site, they would remain responsible for overseeing the daily care we provide our patients. I would reassign the COOs at these facilities to play the horizontal roles. All these COOs would be detached from their local facilities and given the new title of corporate vice president, reporting to one of three corporate senior vice presidents. Their job was to identify variations in practice across all of Scripps and work with the local CEOs and management teams to implement a single, standard "best practice" wherever possible. Within the local facilities, departments would now report to not just one boss, but two—the local on-site CEO and the corporate vice president. To replace the local COOs without adding substantial costs, I promoted the chief nurses at these sites and gave them operational responsibility as well as the title of chief nursing and operations executive.

It was a radical rethinking of the management structure at Scripps, and unprecedented in our industry. Would our people go for it? The CEOs at our hospitals saw the wisdom of standardizing processes at Scripps, but they weren't thrilled about sharing power with the corporate vice presidents. Our corporate leaders were open to the idea but uncertain about trying something that hadn't been done elsewhere. Ultimately, some in our organization embraced the idea while others opposed it. But we couldn't afford to wait around until we achieved universal consensus; we had to act, and we did, realizing that the transition might be messy and we'd have to learn from our mistakes.

As part of an initiative that we labeled "One Scripps," we brought all our former COOs who had been spread throughout the system and gave them a new office. Actually, we gave them the space for an office but no desks, executive assistants, or anything like that. They needed to figure out how to organize themselves and, more important, how to coordinate with their "vertical" counterparts. As I told them, I wanted them to sustain a constructive tension with the vertical executives on site, collaborating to bridge communication gaps and arrive at common solutions. For any given practice, the vertical CEOs would say, "This is how *we* do it." And the corporate vice presidents would say, "We can't have five or more different practices across Scripps." Working together, they could arrive at a single solution that local leaders felt they could implement.

Our new hybrid model experienced some bumps at first as people got used to it, but we saw results almost immediately. For instance, a system-wide audit of respiratory equipment found that each facility had been renting an increased number of medical ventilators. Rented equipment cost Scripps an average of $365,000 annually—or $1,000 a day—without any benefit to patients. The respiratory therapy team knew they needed to reassess this process, so they analyzed costs to see if purchasing the equipment could save money. "We determined that if we purchased the equipment instead of renting it, within two years we could be saving Scripps $300,000 each and every year," said Rebecca Cofinas, corporate vice president of operations, clinical support. "We will invest these critical dollars in other projects that are value added by improving the quality of care and the patient experience." Under our new system, each facility would have more ventilators on site. "It was only when we looked at this as a system versus individual sites that this huge opportunity became apparent," Cofinas added. "This is a real-life example of the power of working as a team."[7]

Many other initiatives quickly got under way. We integrated operations of radiation therapy teams. We adopted policies for keeping up the physical plants—for instance, standardizing how we monitor and adjust the temperature and humidity. We standardized security guard training. Our pharmacies centralized their purchasing, negotiating favorable new contracts with vendors. Overall, thanks to dozens of such initiatives, we produced $77 million in cost savings in 2011, an additional $64 million in 2012, and $83 million in 2013. That's $224 million of waste taken out of our system—achieved while also improving quality, increasing patient satisfaction, and sustaining our high Great Place to Work scores among employees. As these results suggest, joint decision making and the sharing of information can accomplish so much when deployed proactively through well-designed management structures.[8] Knowledge really is power—especially when it's shared.

Engender Collaboration Proactively Throughout the Ranks

While our hospital CEOs and corporate vice presidents were working on administrative and operational issues, we mobilized our medical experts to address variations in the way we care for patients suffering from specific conditions. We asked ourselves: If our four hospitals are responsible for $150 million of wasteful variation, what kinds of efficiencies might we reap if we reexamined the ways our 2,600 affiliated doctors practice medicine? There were numerous disparities in how doctors in the same specialty used equipment, dispensed medications, evaluated patients, and so on. Not all medical practice could be standardized without compromising the care of individual patients, but much of it could be, and as we saw with our emergency rooms, standardization could actually improve the patient experience. As our chief medical officer quipped, we needed to move from "eminence based medicine"—in which doctors treated patients in their own idiosyncratic ways, citing their own professional authority as justification—to "evidence based medicine" that would derive best practices from objective data. There was necessary variation and unnecessary variation; we needed to keep the former and remove the latter.

Our chief medical officer calculated that standardizing medical practice could save us as much as $300 million a year. To identify suitable opportunities for standardization, we added to our new hybrid management structure a process for bringing physicians and administrators together to create standardized care systems. We called these "clinical care lines" and created eight of them: cardiology, oncology, orthopedics, diabetes, behavioral health, neurosciences, primary care, and women's and newborn. To oversee each one, we took a physician leader from each hospital campus and a system-wide physician leader and teamed them with a system-wide administrator and a local administrator. These individuals were asked to "co-manage," narrowing the gap of communication and ideally arriving at collaborative, "best-practice" solutions that we could adopt system-wide. They would lead physicians within these care lines to evaluate and standardize specific medical procedures.

Physician/administrative co-management has proven extraordinarily effective, resulting in a number of exciting innovations that enhance the value of the care we deliver. In 2011, we brought together pathologists and administrators to standardize the ways our medical labs operate. As a result, patients in need of tests now need call only one number to learn about available lab appointments anywhere in our system (formerly they had to place multiple calls). We save money by bringing back in-house procedures we used to outsource to other vendors—something we can do because we're now sharing our personnel and equipment resources. In-house testing also improves quality and speeds up test results. These results are now entered into a single database rather than two, allowing for easy entry into the patient's electronic medical record. In addition, technical committees we've convened have reviewed each lab test we provide, taking every opportunity to standardize the tools and procedures we use.[9]

Cardiology is another area where co-management has made a difference. One cardiac surgeon discovered that he was using a drug, nitric oxide, at one hospital but not at another hospital. Comparing how the patients fared in each case, we found no difference in outcome. Eliminating this drug from our treatment protocol saved $500,000 a year. Our analyses of different drugs and procedures saved additional funds while improving patient care or at the very least leaving it unaffected.

Working together, we've also changed the way we rehabilitate patients at Scripps. At Scripps Mercy Hospital, it used to be that trauma patients needing rehabilitation before being discharged were sent outside of Scripps—even though one of our hospitals, Scripps Encinitas, is nationally known for its rehab facilities. To remedy this situation, we brought together a number of key players from both campuses: physicians, nurses, case managers, and financial staff, among others. Our mission was to figure out how to transfer patients from Mercy to Encinitas in a way that was both safe and efficient. Some patients who finish their rehab at Encinitas continue their recovery at home using Scripps therapists, and when they're able, they move on to outpatient rehab at one of our clinics.[10]

A final example of co-management at work is our redesign of inpatient care at our hospitals. Patients are often anxious about their conditions when they arrive, and the experience of staying in a hospital can be confusing. Our redesigned protocol, rolled out at all hospital sites, assigns each patient a "navigator" who works side by side with physicians, coordinating care and handling patient questions and concerns. Each day, doctors, nurses, the navigator, and other team members conduct rounds with patients and their families. The navigator facilitates to make sure all aspects of care are considered. Throughout the day, the care team members work together to implement the care plan for the patient.

"This new model of care helps me create a more predictable, well-defined care environment for our patients," one of our nurses reported. "The care we're providing is much more timely and manageable and it's much more goal oriented." This nurse adds that patients feel "more relaxed and . . . more secure because their care is tangible. They not only hear about it, but they see it with the regular presence of their care team."[11]

You may wonder whether doctors would have resisted such standardization efforts, perceiving them as diminishing their ability to make independent, professional judgments. Some have taken issue with specific medical decisions we've made system-wide, but overall they have strongly embraced our efforts to redesign our care lines. That's because *they* have played a large part in making key decisions. We as administrative leaders are not telling doctors to do this or that in order to save money; we're inviting them to work with us to arrive at a solution that's best for patients, one that secondarily, by reducing needless variation, will save the organization money. Once we've bridged the information gap and shown doctors data suggesting that a specific course of treatment is better than the alternatives, they usually move on their own to change their behavior. The last thing they want to do is provide care that is inconsistent with best practices or the care of other physicians.

Co-management between front-line physicians and administrators has worked so well that we are extending it beyond the redesign of care lines to the everyday running of our ambulatory medical clinics. Traditionally, medical departments like oncology or cardiology were headed by a physician of that same specialty; we've put an administrator in charge as well to handle hiring, scheduling, and other management issues. The physician leader may want to restrict the number of patients the department handles, to maximize the time doctors spend with them. The administrator may be receiving complaints from patients about the long wait for appointments. The two leaders have valid, although differing points of view. Working together through the differences and bridging the information gap, the two can each make concessions and come up with a scheduling plan that provides the best patient quality and experience.

We're continuing to pioneer new structures that bring physicians and administrators together. Remember the Leadership Academy we created for our middle managers? In 2011, we created a Physicians Leadership Academy (PLA) to help us develop future physician leaders. Like Leadership Academy proper, PLA gives senior leaders—both physician and administrative—a chance to share and model our cultural values of accountability, transparency, "managing down," and collaboration. It also gives me and senior management a chance to build personal relationships with physicians. In fact, one young doctor who attended PLA approached me and asked me to be his mentor. I agreed, and we discovered that we actually had similar backgrounds and career challenges, even though he is originally from South America. It is not the norm in health care for administrators to mentor younger physicians in management, but by institutionalizing the principle of proactive collaboration, we've opened the way for all kinds of positive outcomes we never could have envisioned.

Take Your Time

Our drive to cut out waste has been so successful that more than seventy organizations in our industry have contacted us to learn more about it, and the Advisory Board Company (a global research, technology, and consulting firm that helps hospital and university executives better serve patients and students) has named our "matrix" management structure a national best practice. We encourage others to use what we've done, and we think organizations beyond health care can benefit by creating structures for people in different domains, functions, specialties, or geographies to tackle problems together. In every organization there arise tensions that, when channeled properly, can power innovation and growth. An example is the traditional divide between strategic planning experts, who want to take risks and move a company ahead, and executives in finance, who are typically more risk-averse. To manage a company well, you don't need strategy or finance; you need *both* perspectives in a constructive tension. You need competent, intelligent professionals exchanging views and constructing a course of action they both own.

Does that sound idealistic? I'm not suggesting you can simply erect a new management structure and think you'll solve all your problems overnight. One small hospital system that contacted us came back a year later complaining that they had adapted our collaborative model and hadn't seen any results. They tried to get physicians to work with administration, and some of the doctors had balked. As I explained to the leaders of this health care system, management structures in and of themselves don't bring about results. *People* do—aided by structures. Our matrix model was able to work because we had spent a decade building up relationships of all kinds at Scripps, especially those that crossed the traditional divide between doctors and administrators. Beginning back in 2000 with our Physicians Leadership Cabinet, we had slowly but surely embedded collaboration, transparency, and the bridging of communication gaps into our culture, so that when I introduced the concept of our matrix model, it didn't seem entirely foreign or without precedent.

To bring people together, proceed incrementally. Don't worry if some people in your organization don't "play ball" at first. Collaborate with those who are open to it. As more decisions get made and as you notch some successes, you'll gain momentum and build trust. It takes time to heal poisoned relationships, but it can and does happen. Over time, conflicts that once were divisive and emotionally charged will fade into the background. At Scripps, we never thought that administrators and front-line physicians would sit together in the same room jointly making critical organizational decisions. Yet eventually they did—and still do.

The truth is that people in conflict have more in common than they think. In health care, doctors have traditionally thought that administrators care only about making money; administrators have countered that doctors are naïvely unconcerned with money. In fact, most administrators I know care deeply about patients, and most doctors care at least somewhat about the financial health of the hospital or clinic where they practice. As front-line leaders, we need to elevate our organizations, helping front-line staff and executives overcome their egos and make decisions that benefit the organization, not just a particular interest group. We need to bring our people together for the good of those we ultimately serve: our patients and customers.

Taking Action

To bring people together:

- Create structures that allow you to bring distrustful parties together to bridge the gap of information.
- Share informal power rather than dictating solutions.

- Create formal mechanisms that encourage collaborative decision making—up to and including new management and reporting structure.
- Implement co-management as an operating principle, even on the front lines.
- Start slow and build incrementally on your successes. Overcoming conflict and building trust takes time, but it can happen.

Chapter Ten

Ask "What If?"

B ig changes are under way in health care. Within the next few years, if you want to consult with your doctor, you won't always call his or her office as you do today, make an appointment, and come in for a visit in a few weeks' or months' time. That's so twentieth century. Instead, you'll experience health care in the comfort of your own home. Your consultation, in many cases, will take place by e-visit or video conference. Devices and smartphone applications will allow doctors to take your blood pressure and perform EKG tests on you remotely. If you suffer from a chronic illness, health care professionals will be able to monitor your condition in real time from a central location, just as security services have done for years with your home. Eventually—and don't be bothered by this—you'll have microscopic devices inside your body that monitor your health on a cellular level, detecting cancer and other serious illnesses long before you ever get sick, and sending results wirelessly to your doctor. We won't dispense with office visits completely, because there will remain many situations in which the doctor's direct human touch remains indispensable. But a significant portion of your health care will take place wirelessly and over the Internet, just as banking and shopping do today.

As with any important technological shift, wireless medicine will not come without a certain amount of resistance or controversy. Some physicians, hospitals, and health care systems will decry threats to "the way we've always done things" and resist change. Others will embrace change, but only when adoption of the technology has gone mainstream, leaving them scrambling to catch up. At Scripps, we've been leading in wireless medicine research. In 2009, we became a founding affiliate of the West Wireless Health Institute, a pathbreaking organization dedicated to taking wireless health technologies from bench to bedside, for better patient care at a lower cost. Scripps Health Chief Academic Officer Dr. Eric Topol, a national expert in cardiology and the future of medicine, has remarked, "Not only does [wireless medicine] fit the optimal models of individualized and consumer-driven health care, but there is tremendous potential to upgrade quality of care, reduce the cost burden, and shift away from reactive to preventive medicine."[1] Although we still have far to go, we've already begun testing wireless monitoring devices in clinical settings. In 2013, our Scripps Green Hospital launched a pilot project with more than two dozen patients using a wireless monitoring device worn around the wrist to monitor a full set of vital signs.[2] We've since expanded our testing to a second hospital.

And that's just the beginning. Imagine pocket ultrasound units that doctors can use instead of more expensive fixed ultra-sound units. Or technology that lets doctors see vital signs, lab reports, and other patient data on their tablets or smartphones. Or a device that allows diabetic patients to monitor and send their blood sugar level readings wirelessly. Or another device, the size of a cookie, that, when you hold it against your forehead for ten seconds, tells you your pulse, temperature, respiration, oxygen saturation, and blood pressure. Or still another smartphone-based device that analyzes your breath and can tell you if you have lung cancer. These technologies aren't five or ten years into the future; we're testing and using them now.

Innovation and a general openness to change are a critical part of front-line leadership. If you care about your people, you must discipline yourself to think long term and big picture, because only the organization's long-term survival can ensure job security. Don't just spout glib talk about "seeing around the corner"; take time to imagine the road ahead and compare your own leadership capacities with those that will be required. Invest meaningful resources in preparing yourself, your team, and your organization for potential developments, including any catastrophes that could occur. Engage everyone in becoming nimbler and more efficient, working proactive change processes deep into the organization's DNA. Whenever possible, keep well ahead of market trends and shifting customer needs, even if this means taking risks not everyone understands or agrees with. Lead courageously and decisively, challenging the organization to move past what is already comfortable.

If you're serious about connecting with, serving, and protecting front-line staff, there's a two-word question you should constantly be asking yourself: "What if?"

Make Contingency Planning a Way of Life

Too many leaders avoid asking this question, particularly as it applies to potentially disastrous disruptions of the business. Traditional management wisdom doesn't emphasize speculative, future-oriented thinking. Instead, it conceives of leaders as pragmatists focused on handling what's directly in front of us. It's easy to get distracted, we're told, when we close our eyes and contemplate what the business and the industry might be. Yet to my mind the real danger lies in *not* thinking about future possibilities and contingencies, because if you don't take time to imagine the future, you have no hope of proactively addressing possible threats. We see it all the time: the more success an organization enjoys, the more it becomes comfortable, risk-averse, smug, arrogant, and tone-deaf. Leaders assume that what worked in the past will continue to work. About potential disasters, they think, *Oh, that could never happen to us!* But of course, disasters do sometimes materialize. And when they do, leaders get caught by surprise, with fewer levers available for them to pull.

Guess who usually pays the price in these situations? Not leaders. *Front-line workers.* Let's say you're a manager responsible for staffing a department of a hospital. You know, based on your projections, that you'll have a large number of patients, so you've hired a full complement of staff to take care of them. But for some reason, the patients don't come through the door. During one week, only 60 percent of your beds are filled, and you were expecting 90 percent. What do you do?

Your first response is likely denial. *Oh,* you think, *this is just a fluke. I don't need to worry. The numbers will bounce right back.*

But they don't. Two weeks go by. Three. And still the occupancy is 60 percent. Now your operating margin is dropping fast. Another week goes by, and you're at 58 percent. Now you're losing money.

Uh-oh, you think, *I've got a problem. I need to do something.*

The challenge in health care, as in many industries, is that you can't take strong action unilaterally. You need buy-in from superiors and employees. So you call some meetings to try to fix the problem quickly. That doesn't go so well. It's not easy getting all the relevant decision makers in one room at the same time. The clock is ticking, and your losses are getting bigger and bigger.

Now three months have gone by. You've managed to come up with a plan that people agree on. But by now you're at only 45 percent occupancy, and you're losing much more money than you had been initially. The plan you devised won't make much of a difference anymore. You need to do something radical. You look at the numbers again. Your biggest cost by far is labor. If you're going to make your financial goals, the only solution is to lay people off. So that's what you do.

Layoffs often stem from a particular kind of leadership failure—a lack of *vision.* Organizations that feel they must lay off employees often reach that point because they failed to imagine what might happen. They focus on making their short-term numbers, assuming that the future will just "take care of itself." When it doesn't, they flounder until they have no choice but lay people off. Workers and their families suffer on account of leadership's arrogant neglect.

The best thing about asking "What if?" is that you put yourself in a position where you don't have to ask: "Now what?" Before I came to Scripps, my job was essentially to handle "Now what?" situations. By default, police officers are tasked with figuring out what to do once threats or dangers had already materialized. Later, as I rose through the ranks in health care, I specialized in turning around dysfunctional and failing organizations—businesses where *everyone* was asking "Now what?" When I arrived at Scripps in 1999, it was mired in "Now what?" thinking. Planning for the future was impossible when we had barely enough cash to pay our bills, we didn't know the full state of our finances, key people and groups in the organization weren't talking to one another, employee morale was low, and community support for our organization was waning.

Even as we dealt with the day-to-day business of turning Scripps around, we began to prepare the organization for disasters *before* they happened. Our mobile emergency field hospitals, for instance, were designed to protect our staff and communities in case of earthquakes, floods, terrorism, and other disasters. The unthinkable had happened in lower Manhattan; it could happen in San Diego, too. In 2012, we took our preparedness even further by forming an antiterrorism task force at Scripps, partnering with local police and sheriff departments to evaluate risks and prepare for bomb threats, shootings, and other situations. We're also the first hospital system in the country to have lockboxes containing keys that law enforcement can use to gain entry to the facilities in case of a Columbine-style shooting incident. In an active shooter situation, officers can go right in instead of waiting for a SWAT team to arrive, ideally preventing more casualties. We fervently hope that a shooting or hostage situation will never break out, but just in case, we have a solid plan in place to protect our employees and patients.

We've also implemented contingency planning in the running of our operations. Our project management group came online in 2002 as a quick-response team in case parts of our business went horribly wrong or just needed help. In 2008, we were one of the first in health care to implement an extensive enterprise risk management process as part of our strategic planning process. Collecting extensive data via surveys, interviewing, and group meetings, we created a large inventory of organizational, departmental, and project-related risks. At the organizational or enterprise level, we created a list of the top ten risks we faced. We updated it in 2010 and 2013, and the list changed significantly with each update—confirming the need for a continuous, proactive monitoring of risks.

In our local facilities, we encourage middle managers to track risks and frame thoughtful contingency plans with their own hospitals when patient volumes fluctuate. Managers then put into action previously devised adjustments in staffing and support services. Standardization of nursing practices further improves our response, giving us another, more fiscally attractive option (we can confidently and effectively move nurses and other staff around our system). With smart contingency planning, small problems stay small, and we never get to a point where we have to make radical changes that cost people their jobs.

As I tell our managers, the Department of Defense doesn't wait to be attacked before designing a plan to defend the country. I'll bet they even have plans in place in case we are attacked through Canada. Now, what's the likelihood of that happening? Pretty small. But our military probably has a plan in place anyway. As business leaders, we must deliver a similar degree of preparedness. We should have detailed plans for worst-case scenarios, even those we doubt we'll ever see. As the saying goes, the best contingency plan you'll ever have is the one you'll never use.

Not long ago, I was giving a speech, and a gentleman in the back raised his hand. He said, "I used to work for the defense department, and there *is* a plan for Canada."

I rest my case.

Address Big-Picture Threats

You can apply contingency planning to specific parts of your operations, but the real payback comes when you apply it to your entire business. This unfolds in stages—at least, it did for us. Initially we were focused simply on stabilizing our operations and healing our organization. But by about 2005, Scripps was moving in the right direction. Conflict had cooled, our finances were stronger, quality of care was up, and employee morale was brightening. Surprisingly, that good news left us asking: "Now what?" Did our team have the necessary skills and competencies to lead Scripps as a successful and growing business? I suggested to my colleagues that if we were to continue to succeed we needed to move away from our reactive, crisis mentality and open ourselves up to new, long-term ways of thinking and acting.

We did exactly that. We began to develop long-term strategic plans that called for building out the culture at Scripps, developing our Leadership Academy, making improvements based on the Great Place to Work survey, enhancing employee benefits, luring new talent to the organization and retaining the great people we already had, strengthening financial performance and patient quality, making sensible acquisitions, and coming together around missions like aiding the Hurricane Katrina survivors. Our finances steadily improved, and our organization continued to expand. This in turn brought us to another inflection point. In 2010, when we were designing our new horizontal management structure, we realized that our task was no longer just to run a strong business. It was also to anticipate the long-term threats lining up before us and to take preventative action, even if this meant doing things that health care systems hadn't done before.

Wireless technologies were on the horizon, and so were the financially disruptive effects of health care reform. Our present way of delivering care was unsustainable—not just for us, but for the country, too. If Scripps did nothing, we'd wake up in a few years and find ourselves like Kodak—outdated and uncompetitive. It was far better to seize the initiative and innovate; that way, we would turn threats into potential opportunities. And we couldn't just launch one, isolated initiative. With health insurance reimbursements projected to decline, we had to question the very fundamentals of our business. We had always organized care around the capital-intensive, physical infrastructure of hospitals. Was that really the way health care would be delivered in the future, or would it be delivered less expensively and efficiently across an entire, integrated health care *system*? We still operated in silos; this made some of our doctors, staff, and managers happy, but would it be affordable three to five years from now? We needed to look at the organization horizontally to take costs out, but more fundamentally, we needed to evolve the organization into one that was willing to take risks. We couldn't just copy someone else's success pattern. We needed to create a *new* success pattern, even if that meant radically departing from our existing practices and structures.

By 2012, our organization had largely accepted horizontal management and the project of standardization and reducing variation. Everyone could see where the industry was headed. Yet leadership had continued to look into the future, and we were finding that reducing wasteful variation wasn't enough to keep Scripps viable. First, health care reform would hit our revenues even harder than we initially thought; the few hundred million in cost savings we'd achieved through standardization wouldn't be enough to sustain us financially. Second, our care delivery structures and processes were out of date, rendering the practice of medicine far less joyful and efficient than it had been. People were working harder than ever, but they were spending most of their time on bureaucratic tasks that didn't add value for patients and that felt like drudgery. Some nurses and doctors were devoting only two to four hours of a twelve-hour shift to actually caring for patients! Standardization had been the low-hanging fruit, and it had applied to only specific departments or clinical operations; what we needed to do now was overhaul our *entire* system of delivering care, addressing multiple departments and clinical operations. We needed to pioneer a new work environment for front-line personnel, one designed purposely to add value.

Our chief medical officer, Dr. Jim LaBelle, suggested we call this initiative "Value by Design." I loved that name because it indirectly conveyed the truth about our present inefficient system, which had evolved over time by accident. Modern health care practices were developed with providers in mind, not patients. And they were developed randomly and inconsistently, with all kinds of bureaucracy separating units and departments from one another. Have you ever been to an old European city with its narrow, winding roads and neighborhoods built next to one another with no particular rhyme or reason? That's what U.S. health care is like—overly complex, meandering, disorienting, almost indecipherable. Like old cities, our health care system was never planned out in a neat, logical fashion. Patients go through the hospital interacting with all sorts of different departments, but each one has its own set of rules and regulations, adding unnecessary cost and risk. Our task with Value by Design was to knock down our "city," block by block, and build it up again so it's easier for patients to find their way through.

As of 2014, a number of Value by Design projects are completed and more are under way, using lean process-improvement methodologies. Remember our emergency room redesign? That early, transitional project inspired a number of similar Value by

Design redesigns—some of which I described in Chapter Nine in connection with our co-management model. We perform "rapid cycle redesigns," bringing all stakeholders together for an intensive week in which we share perspectives on our existing practice, identify areas of waste, and design a future practice. We have changed how our nurses perform assessments on patients in our hospitals, cutting the time nurses must spend on meaningless paperwork by thirty minutes for each patient. We've designed a new process of handling patients from the moment they walk into the emergency department until thirty days after they exit inpatient care, cutting waste by planning from the very beginning. In our operating rooms, we've redesigned our processes to improve how promptly we start the first surgeries each day and by standardizing the ways we purchase, stock, and deliver supplies. Even more system redesigns are kicking off all the time.

Continuous process improvement through lean methodologies is by no means new, but it is only recently being applied at health care organizations. There was far less incentive to make such process improvements during the 1980s and 1990s, since few people saw a reason to change; organizations could always count on government, private insurers, and patients to pump more money into the system. What prompted change for us was the realization that this money just wasn't forthcoming any longer. In fact, if we didn't change we'd get *less* money and would go out of business. As I told our people, the good old days were over, but even better days lay ahead.

Rally Your People

Front-line staff and physicians play a critical role in lean processes, as they're the ones who know best where the waste is and how to eliminate it. As our early experience has shown, staff who participate in redesign projects come away energized by the experience. During our operating room redesign, a group of medical technicians thanked managers for finally asking for their input. They had known all along about causes of waste and inefficiency, such as supplies that were opened but never used and simply thrown away. They wanted to add more value, but the organization had never asked them to help take the whole system apart and put it back together again. It was gratifying and even somewhat a relief that it was finally happening.

Buoyed by this early feedback, we've been working to mobilize the entire organization behind Value by Design, educating staff about the bigger-picture issues we face and helping them understand how they personally participate to make Scripps better. We're in the process of training all executives in lean processes, which entails an investment of hundreds of thousands of dollars. We've also created a ninety-minute interactive activity introducing Value by Design, which we're rolling out to every one of our 13,500 employees. Called "Excellence All Around You," the activity leads employees through an animated discussion of our vision and strategies, deliberately applying many of the principles I've discussed in this book. We draw on our middle managers, assigning over 125 Leadership Academy alumni to lead the conversation. The activity's content builds on our commitment to employee advocacy by inviting them to play a strong role in shaping organizational change. We do this by telling employees we want them to become thought leaders, share expertise, show courage in exposing challenges or weaknesses, and take ownership of solutions. We present continuous improvement as "changing from a method of 'firefighting' and 'top-down' management" to a process of "purposeful change" and daily self-management of operations by employees. We also stress accountability, sharing patient satisfaction scores for hospital and outpatient care settings. By making the presentation a conversation as opposed to a lecture, we stress collaboration between management and teams of nurses, physicians, and other front-line staff. And by sharing corporate strategies and the external forces facing our organization, we attempt to bridge information gaps and bring everyone together behind the effort to reach our common goals.

Perhaps the principle most evident in the presentation is storytelling. The discussion is organized around a colorful kit resembling a board game with flashcards and a large map that depicts where our organization currently is and where we want to take it. Reading the map from the bottom up, employees understand that we're currently an organization encumbered by waste, redundancy, non-value-added activity, and narrow patient access to our services. On top of that we wish to build a new, better Scripps organized around the patient. This organization will integrate all forms of care, drive innovation, and feature better teamwork and collaboration across silos. The map frames meaning by presenting change as a mountain we're all climbing together, with the "winds of change" blowing all around it.

So far, response to the activity has been outstanding. Employees enjoy the conversation and express their eagerness to help participate in Value by Design. A patient transport specialist said, "You know I work two jobs—both at hospitals—and I am proud to be at Scripps. I think this new program is going to make things so much better. I tell my patients that Scripps is the best and if we all do what this program says, we will be the best." Leadership Academy alumnus Rob Sills reports that

> the stories [workers] talked about and shared around the table while they looked at the visualization were personal and inspiring. Many of our staff would comment about how a particular scene makes them feel or they would relate a story that happened to them or a loved one. The power of this exercise is the conversations that occur around the roadmap. As facilitators, all we have to do is start the conversation, the team does the rest. At the end of each session, the staff all have asked the same question: What can we do now to help get Scripps to the top scene on the map?[3]

Many CEOs in our industry have responded to the changing health care landscape by taking early retirement. The challenges seem too great to them. We view the future differently. With "Excellence All Around You," our leadership team stands in front of our employees and says, "This is the *best* time ever in health care. It is going to be a rewarding, exciting time. We know health care is broken, and those that are willing to help redesign a health care delivery system—literally take out a blank piece of paper and redesign the entire system—are going to thrive." With our people behind Value by Design, I know we'll succeed. Will we be at the top of the map three years from now? I can't say for sure, but I'm both optimistic and willing to be patient.

Like the cultural change I've described in previous chapters, remaking our basic work processes takes time. And as a former cop, I'm aware of the dangers of charging ahead too fast. One story I like to tell our staff is of a time when I had just gotten my badge and was a bit too enthralled with the power I had been given. A call came in for me to assist another officer in responding to a burglary in progress. I was nearby, so I turned on my emergency lights and blew through an intersection—nearly colliding with the car of the officers I was supposed to assist. I could have killed us all. While it's important to get somewhere quickly, the *most* important thing is to get there in one piece. A bit of caution is in order in law enforcement, business, and life. If you perish trying to grasp a desired future, you don't do anyone any good.

Sadly, I saw that lesson played out before me when I came to Scripps. A turnaround of the organization had been necessary in the first place because the previous CEO had tried to reform the organization long before it was ready. This CEO was brilliant, and he was convinced his path was the right one, so he plunged straight ahead. I remember telling him once how I had almost been killed responding to that burglary call, and he said, "Well, that's the trouble with you traditional hospital administrators—you don't have any balls. I'm going to prove to you that I'm right." At the time, I sincerely hoped that he *was* right. A year later, though, he was out of a job. He came into my office as he was leaving and said, "I crashed, didn't I?"

"Yeah," I responded. "I think you did. And unfortunately, the question yet to be answered is how many bodies you will take with you."

Always Fall Up

Even more deadly than speeding too fast toward the future, however, is failing to move toward it at all—a fearful and stubborn clinging to what already exists, and a reluctance to ask, "What if?" Inspired by my time as a cop, I want to urge you to confront any fears you may have about change and to stride boldly ahead. Accidents occur all the time on the streets. Lives are shattered. Jobs are lost. Hopes and dreams come to an end. But in the wake of setbacks, often (although of course not always) people can process the loss and make new beginnings. I call this kind of resiliency "falling up." When I experienced my career-ending injury, I eventually "fell up" and landed in an exciting new career in health care. Scripps also "fell up" following a difficult period of turmoil, becoming an entirely different organization from what people at the time might have ever imagined.

We tend to forget that good things can come out of seemingly dire circumstances and setbacks—that what seems like a threat is often an opportunity in disguise. You see, *all* of us have the ability to "fall up." We can determine our own paths and those of our organizations to an extent far greater than we may realize. Outside forces matter, but we can position ourselves and our organizations to handle what comes at us and even benefit from it. No matter what challenges your organization faces or you personally face as a leader, don't resist change; promote it. Don't fear the future; welcome it in.

Taking Action

To ask "what if?":

- Put contingency plans in place to address threats to local operations. Remember, the most valuable plan is one you never have to use.
- Take long-term strategic planning seriously. Even if you've been successful, never rest on your laurels.
- Make continual improvement an explicit part of your culture.
- Mobilize front-line personnel to participate in innovation and department change initiatives.
- Adopt an attitude of "always falling up."
- Change before you are forced to change.

Conclusion

If you've spent time in the military or law enforcement, you may have heard of challenge coins—medallions given to select individuals honoring a milestone event, special achievement, or valiant action. Different departments or military units each have unique coins imprinted with logos or other design elements. They're called challenge coins because the person you give one to is supposed to carry it around with them at all times. If you later run into this person, you can "challenge" them to present their coin. If they don't have the coin on them, they're supposed to buy you a drink. It's a loose tradition, of course; I've never known a recipient who has been challenged, much less made to buy a drink. The point is simply to recognize someone who merits it.

Some years back, I decided to create a challenge coin with the Scripps logo on it to present to employees who performed exemplary service. The first one I gave out was to Dwight Johnson, a young security guard at Scripps Memorial Hospital La Jolla. Scripps La Jolla has a chemical dependency treatment program. This isn't a "locked" facility; if someone wants to leave during their treatment for drug or alcohol addiction, they can do so. In 2009, Johnson was on duty in the middle of the night, much as I had been so many years earlier. A patient in the chemical dependency program had had enough of treatment and left the unit. Johnson, acting on his own initiative, found the patient before he left our campus. Although Johnson didn't have to, he spent hours talking to the man, trying to convince him not to give up on getting sober. Eventually, the patient agreed to go back into the program.

This patient went on to complete the program and, to the best of my knowledge, he has been sober ever since. Every six months or so, he connects with Johnson to say hello, stay in touch, and express his gratitude. The man calls Johnson his "angel" and credits him with saving his life. When I heard about what Johnson did, I was so impressed that I went down to the emergency department, where Johnson usually works, and gave him a challenge coin in front of a number of physicians, nurses, and other colleagues.

Presenting an employee with a personal gift for outstanding service might not seem like such a big deal, but the impact it has is enormous. When the CEO of a sizeable organization takes the time to recognize an employee, people notice. I've since run into Johnson maybe half a dozen times in passing. Each time, he's pulled it out of his pocket to show me before I've even had a chance to challenge him. I feel like I have a different relationship with him than I did before—a closer, more personal connection.

It's true that front-line leadership is more challenging and riskier than conventional approaches. It's risky to get out of the office and ask front-line employees to ask you tough questions. It's risky to invite front-line workers, physicians, and other stakeholders to share leadership roles with you. It's risky to tell personally meaningful stories from your gut. It's risky to mobilize the organization to help in moments of crisis. It's risky to publicly commit to a no-layoff philosophy. But such risks—as well as the investment of personal and organizational resources—are well worth it. The heightened performance you'll see is essential in today's economy, no matter what industry you are in. Even more so, the risk is worth it because the diverse parts of front-line leadership make the leader's role far more personally satisfying than it would otherwise be.

So how do you get started? What can you do *right now*, today, to begin? First, take stock of what you're already doing (and not doing) to engage with employees. You could ask others around you to provide 360-degree evaluations, but it might be even better to analyze your *own* behavior first and ask your team for casual feedback. Once you know where you stand, set a few reasonable, short-term targets for implementing some of the tactics described in this book. Invent "pilot programs" for yourself; for instance, try rolling out weekly Q&A sessions, experimenting with a communication like Market News, or committing to rounding twice a month with employees. Whatever initial actions you take, however modest they may be, *commit to them*. Don't do them halfheartedly, and don't just do them once and forget about them. When it comes to engaging with employees in any of the ways I've discussed, a fly-by is worse than doing nothing at all. Carve the time out of your schedule, and stick to the plan.

For all the effort and attention front-line leadership requires, it isn't especially unfamiliar, novel, or complicated. It's best described as "refreshingly old-fashioned." In our digital world—where life rushes at us 24/7, industries rise and fall in the blink of an eye, and people change jobs numerous times over the course of their lives—doing the hard work of building relationships with your people often seems pointless. There appear to be so many other, more productive ways leaders can spend their time. But we need to rethink that. Relationships still matter—in fact, more than ever. As markets become more volatile, it's even more essential that leaders know *firsthand* the people who are actually carrying the business forward and the work they are doing every day. Technology is wonderful, but it can't solve all of our business challenges. It can't make employees more loyal. It can't align them with an organizational mission. And it can't inspire them to put their utmost effort into their jobs. Only caring, attentive leadership can do these things. To succeed as a leader, borrow this simple lesson from me, a former cop: protect and serve your people.

Notes

Chapter 1

1. Dhanya Skariachan. "Best Buy's New CEO Wants to Learn from the Front Line," Fox Business, September 4, 2012, accessed May 1, 2014, http://www.foxbusiness.com/business-leaders/2012/09/04/best-buy-new-ceo-wants-to-learn-from-front-line/.

Chapter 2

1. I am grateful to our general counsel, Richard Sheridan, for emphasizing this point in a personal email to me, April 21, 2014.

Chapter 3

1. "Special Report: Hurricane Katrina," Scripps internal document.
2. Ibid.
3. Ibid.
4. Ibid.
5. Ibid.
6. "Scripps Medical Response Team, Katrina Mission, Updates and Feedback," Scripps internal document.
7. Ibid.
8. Ibid.
9. Ibid.
10. Cheryl Clark, "Ex-Cop Van Gorder's in the Hot Spot at Scripps," *San Diego Union-Tribune*, June 8, 2000.
11. Chris Van Gorder, "Notes on Haiti—CEO Journal Part 1," Scripps.org, January 22, 2010, accessed May 1, 2014, http://www.scripps.org/news_items/3586-notes-on-haiti-ceo-journal-part-1.

12. Chris Van Gorder, "Notes on Haiti—CEO Journal Part 2," Scripps.org, January 24, 2010, accessed May 1, 2014, http://www .scripps.org/news_items/3587-notes-on-haiti-ceo-journal-part-2.
13. Ibid.
14. Chris Van Gorder, "Notes on Haiti—CEO Journal Part 15," Scripps.org, February 9, 2010, accessed May 1, 2014, http:// www.scripps.org/news_items/3611-notes-on-haiti-ceo-journal -part-15.
15. Chris Van Gorder, "Notes on Haiti—CEO Journal Part 16," Scripps.org, February 9, 2010, accessed May 1, 2014, http://www .scripps.org/news_items/3611-notes-on-haiti-ceo-journal-part-16.
16. Chris Van Gorder, "Notes on Haiti—CEO Journal Part 15."

Chapter 4

1. Patient cases are of course confidential, but Miranda had given us permission to talk publicly about what had happened to her.
2. "The Stroke Had Taken Its Toll on Claire Cordua," Scripps internal document.
3. "Scripps Culture Audit 2, Fortune 100 Best Companies 2014 Application and Supplemental Materials," Scripps internal document, 111.
4. Ibid.
5. Ibid., 60.
6. Ibid., 37.
7. Matthew Gannon, "Exoskeleton Allows Paraplegics to Walk," CNN, March 22, 2013, accessed April 12, 2014, http://www.cnn .com/2013/03/13/tech/innovation/original-ideas-exoskeleton/.

Chapter 5

1. "Scripps Culture Audit 2, Fortune 100 Best Companies 2014 Application and Supplemental Materials," Scripps internal document, 73.
2. Ibid.
3. Yvonne Coombs, email message to author, March 19, 2014.
4. "Scripps Culture Audit 2, Fortune 100 Best Companies 2014 Application and Supplemental Materials," Scripps internal document, 63.
5. Ibid., 62.
6. Fritz Logan, email message to author, March 29, 2014.
7. "Scripps Culture Audit 2, Fortune 100 Best Companies 2014 Application and Supplemental Materials," 61.
8. Inside Scripps, Scripps internal newsletter, August 2012.

9. "Scripps Culture Audit 2," Scripps internal document, 65.
10. *Inside Scripps*, October 2012, 7.
11. "Scripps Culture Audit 2," 66.
12. Ibid., 75.
13. Ibid., 64.
14. Patric Thomas, email message to author, March 26, 2014.
15. "Scripps Culture Audit 2," 68.
16. Lisa Golden, email message to author, March 21, 2014.
17. "Scripps Culture Audit 2," 68.
18. Lisa Golden, email message to author, March 21, 2014.
19. "Scripps Culture Audit 2," 68.
20. Ibid., 70.
21. Ibid., 93.
22. Interview with Paul Randolph, March 20, 2014.
23. Interview with Tarane Sondoozi, March 20, 2014.
24. "Changing Lives Quotes," Scripps internal document, June 8, 2011.
25. "Scripps Culture Audit 2," 84.
26. The latter figure dates from 2010, the most recent year when industry figures were available.
27. Ann Bares, "2011 Turnover Rates by Industry," Compensation force.com, October 26, 2011, accessed April 12, 2014, http://www .compensationforce.com/2011/10/2011-turnover-rates-by -industry.html.

Chapter 6
1. Tragically, incidents like this keep happening. In 2009, a man and his wife were both fired from their jobs at a hospital. The man came home one day and killed himself, his wife, and their five children. Rebecca Cathcart and Randal C. Archibold, "Man Kills His Wife and 5 Children," *New York Times*, January 28, 2009, accessed April 10, 2014, http://www.nytimes.com /2009/01/28/us/28family.html?_r=0&pagewanted=print New York Times.
2. Don Stanziano, email message to author, April 3, 2014.
3. Ibid.
4. Ibid.
5. "Leading the Scripps Way," Scripps internal document.
6. "Building a Culture of Accountability from Within: The Transformation of Scripps Health," A Good Governance Case Study, February 2014, 90. Veronica Zaman, email message to the author, April 22, 2014.
7. Ibid., 90.

8. Ibid., 114–115.
9. Ibid., 110.
10. Ibid., 117.
11. Ibid., 122.
12. Helen Neppes, email message to author, April 3, 2014.
13. "Building a Culture of Accountability from Within," 118.
14. I've changed Nadya's name as well as certain identifying details in this story to protect confidentiality.

Chapter 7

1. "Building a Culture of Accountability from Within: The Transformation of Scripps Health," A Good Governance Case Study, February 2014.
2. Ibid.
3. Ibid.
4. Ibid.
5. Ibid.
6. Dictionary.com. "Accountability." Accessed May 1, 2014, http://dictionary.reference.com/browse/accountability?s=t.
7. Tom Gammiere, email message to the author, April 11, 2014.
8. Ibid.
9. Barbara Price, email message to the author, April 13, 2014.
10. "Building a Culture of Accountability from Within," 140–141.
11. Ibid., 138.
12. Ibid., 139.
13. "Leading the Scripps Way," Scripps internal document.

Chapter 8

1. Helen Neppes, email message to author, March 30, 2014. See also: "Mexico Crash: 16 Killed in Head-On Collision on Caborca-Sonoyta Highway," *Huffington Post*, August 6, 2012, accessed May 3, 2014, http://www.huffingtonpost.com/2012/08/06/mexico-crash_n_1749780.html.
2. Catherine Fay, email message to author, March 29, 2014.
3. Peter Mabrey, email message to author, April 3, 2014.
4. "Leading the Scripps Way," Scripps internal document.
5. "Letters to Our Leader, Scripps Leadership Academy, 2002–2011," Scripps internal document.
6. Johan Otter, email message to author, May 4, 2014.
7. Jorge Murguía, *Inside Scripps*, Scripps internal newsletter.
8. Wendy J. Vaughn, email message to author, March 30, 2014.
9. "Letters to Our Leader."

Chapter 9

1. Jim Molpus, "An Emergency Redesign," *Healthleaders Media Break-throughs* (2011), 25–28.
2. For more on our ER redesign, see GQ Sharieff et al., "Improving Emergency Department Time to Provider, Left-Without-Treatment Rates, and Average Length of Stay," *J Emerg Med* 2013 Sep;45(3):426–32. doi:10.1016/j.jemermed.2013.03 .014. Epub 2013 Jun 6.
3. Tony Fong, "A Question of Confidence," *San Diego Union Tribune*, May 28, 2000.
4. Tony Fong, "Despite Physicians' Unrest, Scripps Board Backs CEO," *San Diego Union Tribune*, May 4, 2000.
5. Cheryl Clark, "Doctors at Mercy Want Scripps Chief Out," *San Diego Union Tribune*, May 18, 2000.
6. "Building a Culture of Accountability from Within: The Transformation of Scripps Health (H1)," A Good Governance Case Study, February 2014.
7. *Inside Scripps*, July 2011.
8. *Inside Scripps*, February/March 2013.
9. Scripps 2010 Annual Report.
10. Ibid.
11. *Inside Scripps*, August 2012.

Chapter 10

1. Steve Carpowich. "Scripps Takes Leadership Role in Wireless Health Care," Scripps.org, April 8, 2009, accessed May 1, 2014, http://www.scripps.org/news_items/3407-scripps-takes-leadership -role-in-wireless-health-care.
2. Keith Darce. "Scripps Launches Pilot Study of Wireless Vital Signs Device," Scripps.org, December 18, 2013, accessed May 1, 2104, http://www.scripps.org/news_items/4696-scripps-launches-pilot -study-of-wireless-vital-signs-device.
3. Rob Sills, email message to the author, April 5, 2014.

About the Author

As president and CEO of Scripps Health since 2000, Chris Van Gorder, FACHE, has positioned Scripps among the nation's foremost health care institutions. More than 13,500 employees and 2,600 affiliated physicians provide care at Scripps, which has made *Fortune* magazine's "100 Best Companies to Work For" list for seven consecutive years and in 2013 was named by *Becker's Hospital Review* as one of the 100 Great Places to Work in Healthcare. Scripps was also named by AARP as the number one employer in the nation for workers fifty and older—the first California-based company to take top honors. In 2008, Van Gorder and his executive team were named the Top Leadership Team in Health Care for large health systems by *HealthLeaders* magazine. For five consecutive years, he was included on the "100 Most Influential in Health Care" list, compiled by *Modern Healthcare* magazine. In 2011, he was listed as number eighteen.

When Van Gorder was named CEO in 2000, Scripps was losing $15 million a year, and employee and physician confidence had hit bottom. Van Gorder responded with a transparent co-management style and a streamlining of business operations, physician relations, and workplace culture—leading to a landmark turnaround. Since then Scripps has set its sights on regional growth and expansion and the development of innovative patient centered care and processes.

Van Gorder serves as a reserve assistant sheriff in the San Diego County Sheriff's Department responsible for search and rescue and law enforcement reserves, as a licensed emergency medical technician (EMT), and as an instructor for the American Red Cross. He currently serves as a professor in health administration practice at the University of Southern California, on the Board of Councilors of the university's Price School of Public Policy, and on the editorial boards of HealthLeaders and the Governance Institute. Van Gorder has served on the California Commission on Emergency Medical Services (EMSA) and on the U.S. Commission for the United Nations Educational, Scientific and Cultural Organization (UNESCO).

Board certified in health care management and an American College of Healthcare Executives (ACHE) fellow, Van Gorder served as 2010 chairman of the association. His numerous awards include several humanitarian awards, the California Emergency Medical Services Authority Distinguished Service medal, and the ACHE Gold Medal, the highest award bestowed by that organization. Van Gorder received his master's degree in public administration/health services administration at the University of Southern California, completed the Wharton CEO Program at the University of Pennsylvania, and earned his bachelor's degree from California State University, Los Angeles.

Van Gorder lives in San Diego, California. For more information, please visit www.scripps.org.

Index